Studies and documents on cultural policies

In this series:

The serial numbering of titles in this series, the presentation of which has been modified, was discontinued with the volume *Cultural policy in Italy*

Cultural policy
in Romania

Ion Dodu Balan
with the co-operation of the
Directorates of the Council
of Socialist Culture and Education

The Unesco Press
Paris 1975

Published by the Unesco Press,
7 Place de Fontenoy, 75700 Paris
Printed by Imprimerie des
Presses Universitaires de France, Vendôme

ISBN 92-3-101188-X
French edition: 92-3-201188-3

Preface

The purpose of this series is to show how cultural policies are planned and implemented in various Member States.

As cultures differ, so does the approach to them; it is for each Member State to determine its cultural policy and methods according to its own conception of culture, its socio-economic system, political ideology and technical development. However, the methods of cultural policy (like those of general development policy) have certain common problems; these are largely institutional, administrative and financial in nature, and the need has increasingly been stressed for exchanging experiences and information about them. This series, each issue of which follows as far as possible a similar pattern so as to make comparison easier, is mainly concerned with these technical aspects of cultural policy.

In general, the studies deal with the principles and methods of cultural policy, the evaluation of cultural needs, administrative structures and management, planning and financing, the organization of resources, legislation, budgeting, public and private institutions, cultural content in education, cultural autonomy and decentralization, the training of personnel, institutional infrastructures for meeting specific cultural needs, the safeguarding of the cultural heritage, institutions for the dissemination of the arts, international cultural co-operation and other related subjects.

The studies, which cover countries belonging to differing social and economic systems, geographical areas and levels of development, present therefore a wide variety of approaches and methods in cultural policy. Taken as a whole, they can provide guidelines to countries which have yet to establish cultural policies, while all countries, especially those seeking new formulations of such policies, can profit by the experience already gained.

This study was prepared for Unesco by Ion Dodu Balan with the co-operation of the Directorates of the Council of Socialist Culture and Education. The opinions expressed are the author's and do not necessarily reflect the views of Unesco.

Contents

Historical and cultural background

Dwelling in the north-eastern part of the Balkan peninsula, the Romanian people, who are descended from the ancient Geto-Dacian peoples and from the Roman world in general, have been recognized throughout their history as a people with a distinctive spiritual personality which finds expression in a rich and original culture.

Owing to the variety of the landscape, the wealth and diversity of the resources of the subsoil and the immense network of natural channels of communication, enduring relations were established among the inhabitants of the whole country, whose centre is the Transylvanian plateau. A homogeneous civilization developed here in the earliest days—a civilization capable of assimilating successive influences, Scythian, Celtic, Greek and, later, those of immigrant peoples. At the beginning of the second century, Dacia, after a long and heroic resistance, became a Roman province, an outlying stronghold of the Roman Empire against the attacks of the barbarian world, an immense reservoir of natural wealth which was intensively and systematically colonized by settlers from every part of the empire. This intensive colonization and the existence side by side, for over a century and a half, of the Dacians and the Roman or Romanized peoples brought about the Romanization of the Dacian population and led to the use of the Latin language. In the year A.D. 271 the imperial legions, retreating before the Goths, established themselves on the banks of the Danube, but the Romanization process continued among the peoples remaining in the former Dacia, as a result of the many relations with the powerful empire close at hand.

In the succeeding centuries, vulgar Latin (Moeso-Dacian) gradually evolved, while retaining the grammatical structure and basic vocabulary. From the ninth century onwards it became the common language of Romania, subsequently being divided into the Daco-Romanian dialect to the north of the Danube and the Macedo-Romanian, Meglenitic-Romanian and Istro-Romanian dialects to the south of the river. The subsequent evolution of one of these dialects, Daco-Romanian, led to its transformation into a literary and national language—Romanian. Throughout its history, the Romanian language—'the first and most important cultural creation of the Romanian people'[1]—has retained characteristics of ancient Latin. Unlike other Romance languages, it has only regional variations and not widely differing dialects, a fact which, from remote times, has made the

1. Tudor Vianu, 'The Originality of the Romanian Cultural Contribution', *Studii de Literatură Romînă*, p. 561, Bucharest, 1965.

9

Romanian people aware of their national unity and enabled them to develop a common culture, in spite of the disparity of social conditions in the various historical provinces.

The first forms of feudal life emerged under the increasing influence of the Roman world, which, extending to the south of the Danube, was represented at that time by the Byzantine Empire, the latter having established relations with the Christian peoples north of the Danube. The Romanian people's awareness of their unity and Latinity is evidenced primarily by the name 'Romanian', which the Romanians themselves have always used but which was also used by the chroniclers of the time, such as Flavio Biondo and Ennea Silvio Piccolimini. The name given to the first feudal state set up north of the Danube—Tara Românească—is also one of the fundamental factors in its existence. The end of the thirteenth century and the beginning of the fourteenth saw the decline of foreign influence and domination over the territory of the Romanians. Along the Carpathians states began to take shape, leading to the emergence of the Tara Românească (the land of Romania in 1330) and of Moldava (Moldavia in 1359) as independent principalities. In Transylvania, structures that prefigured the first Romanian states had emerged as far back as the tenth century.

The main feature of the social structure of the Romanian population was the *obștea* or peasant community. It was because of the continued existence of these peasant communities during the Middle Ages that popular culture has had such a strong influence throughout the whole of Romanian history. The struggle to defend the land and language of past generations against invasion brought about a unity of purpose in action that was faithfully reflected in the State, whose emergence was due, in the first place, to the firm structure of the organization of rural life into an economic and administrative community. Protected against the feudal states, the characteristics of Romanian culture emerged with increasing clarity, notwithstanding powerful external influences. The Romanian language, which expressed the Romanian people's thoughts, became a powerful factor in their cohesion. In spite of difficult periods, sometimes adversely affecting the development of cultural creation, the Romanian people have expressed themselves throughout the centuries almost exclusively through their creative arts: poetry, song, dance, costume, pottery, tools, peasant architecture, and so on—in short, everything that goes to make up the beauty of Romanian folk art, which still amazes us today on account of the originality and rich variety of its content, its charm and inventiveness. Although there was no written literature in the Romanian language until the sixteenth century, oral literature had already been developed for centuries past; a wealth of oral material had been preserved and handed down from one generation to another. The earliest reference to Romanian folklore is found in the *Legenda Maior Sancti Gerardi*, dating from the eleventh century. Epic masterpieces in verse such as *Miorita, Balada Mînăstirii*

Argesului (Ballad of the Monastery of Arges), the *doina* (anonymous lyric poems) and fairy-tales bear witness, centuries afterwards, to the purity of this tradition. The oldest document in the Romanian language, dated and still preserved today, is a letter written by a *boyar* in Cimpulung in 1521 to Hanas Bekner, mayor of Brașov. The first translations into Romanian of religious texts date from the same or almost the same period; these translations, which were made in the north of the country, were no doubt made because, under the influence of the Reformation, it had been realized that the language of the people should be used for divine worship.

The first book printed in Romanian, a translation of a Lutheran catechism, appeared in Sibiu in 1544. Immediately after this, Romanian printing began to develop rapidly. Works produced towards the middle of the sixteenth century by Archdeacon Coressi and by apprentices were widely disseminated and laid the foundations of the Romanian literary language. From the sixteenth to the eighteenth century, however, while in Western Europe the arts, the sciences and literature made rapid strides as a result of the impetus given by the Renaissance, the development of Romanian culture encountered a series of difficulties. At the time when Christopher Columbus discovered a new world, and Spanish, Italian and English literature were in the 'golden age' of their history, the Romanians had to stand up against the expansionist designs and rapacity of hostile empires, in order to defend and protect the magnificent beginnings of a culture revealed to us by the Voronet frescoes, the architecture of the monastery of Curtea de Arges, the *Invătăturile lui Neagoe Basarab către Fiul său Teodosie* (Counsels of Neagoe Basarab to his Son, Teodosie), the poem *Viata Lumii* (The Life of the World) by the Moldavian chronicler Miron Costin (1633–91) and the work of the great scholar Dimitrie Cantemir (1673–1723), the most important Romanian philosopher and savant of the past, a member of the Academy of Berlin and greatly esteemed by Voltaire.

These 'testing times for our country and for ourselves', as the chronicler Miron Costin put it, were hardly conducive to the development of literature, reading or sculpture. The defenders of the country's frontiers against constant invasion—Ioan de Hunedoara (d. 1456), prince of Transylvania, with the Romanian *voivodes* from Mircea cel Bătrîn (Mircea the Old) (1386–1418) to Stefan cel Mare (Stephen the Great) (1457–1504) and Mihai Viteazul (Michael the Brave) (1593–1601)—were at the same time defending the civilization of Western Europe at the height of the Renaissance. It can thus be said that a great many movements that threatened to destroy the priceless values of the European genius were shattered on the Carpathian peaks. But defensive action created a climate conducive to the safeguarding and preservation of cultural traditions and to the creation of new works. From the end of the eighteenth and beginning of the nineteenth centuries new prospects opened up for Romanian culture. The poet Ienăchiță Văcărescu (1740–97) charged his descendants to 'further the Romanian language and honour their country'. The Transylvanian School—a political and cultural movement inspired by this enlightenment, and represented more specially by the scholars Samuil Micøu (1745–1806), Gheorge Sincai (1754–1816) and Petru Maior (1761–1821), all philologists and historians whose intensive studies were carried out first of all in Transylvanian towns and later in Vienna and Rome—demonstrated by scientific argument the organic, historical and cultural links between the Romanian people and Latin civilization. Subsequent generations of creative artists have manifested a passionate interest in the idea of the continuity and unity of our people and our culture, despite the gaps due to the vicissitudes of history.

The nineteenth century, which aroused national consciousness throughout the whole of Europe, also brought about fundamental changes in the history and culture of the Romanian people. The development of capitalism in the three major historical provinces of Romania—Moldavia, Transylvania and Tara Românească—the influence of the ideas of liberty, equality and fraternity proclaimed by the French Revolution, the revolts among the Romanian people led by Horia in Transylvania (1784) and Tudor Vladimirescu in Tara Românească (1821), and, more than anything else, the 1848 revolution which took place in all three provinces—these were the main events in the history of Romania at that time. In the Danubian principalities culture made rapid strides in every domain: education, science, literature, the press, theatre and music. Strongly-knit political and cultural relations between Romanian intellectuals in all the historical provinces were established and developed. In Bucharest, Jassy, Braşov, Craiova, Oradea, Blaj and other towns, groups of intellectuals agitated first for a single Romanian culture and then for the political unity of the Romanians.

The union of Tara Românească with Moldavia in 1859, during the reign of Alexandru Ioan Cuza, fulfilled the dream of the revolutionary fighters of 1848 and an age-old desire of the people as a whole. This event, which aroused particular enthusiasm among Romanians in Transylvania, was at the same time a most important stage in the process of national cultural development. Liberation from the yoke of the Ottoman Empire in 1877 and the completion of national unity by the union of Transylvania and the Romania of the past in 1918, rewarded the sacrifices made by the people and the patriotic action of many members of the intelligentsia with a view to setting up a national State. Throughout the whole of this period an important part was played by Junimea (Youth), a literary, cultural and political society founded in 1863 and headed by the critic Titu Maiorescu (1840–1917), a remarkable person who always supported the concept of the specificity of art within the context of cultural values.

Another literary group—proof of the growing assertion of the workers' awareness—grew up around *Contemporanul* (The Contemporary), a review with socialist tendencies; its leading spirit was C. G. Gherea (1855–1920), a highly talented critic whose ideas approached socialist realism. Realism, moreover, was the keynote of the most important works produced at this time. At the same time, however, other artistic movements began to take shape: symbolism, whose initiator was the poet Alexandru Macedonski (1845–1920); the *semănătorismul* (the sower), a social movement harking back to the past, which extolled the virtues of the rural traditionalism, its theorist and historian being Nicolae Iorga (1871–1940), one of the most gifted figures in Romanian culture; and *poporanismul* (from the word *popor*, people), a political, ideological and literary movement which contrasted rural and city life in an artificial way. Outstepping the political range of this latter movement, the revue *Viaţa Românească* (Romanian Life) (1906), dominated by the personality of the critic Ibraileanu, who was particularly attracted by the positivism of Taine, published the work of the most eminent writers and scholars of the day, almost all of whom were patriots and democrats. In general, the period between the two wars—a period which saw the appearance on the political and ideological scene of the Romanian Communist Party (founded in May 1921), which had a considerable humanistic and democratic influence—is recognized as being one of the most productive in Romanian history from the point of view of outstanding achievements, marked by the interplay and clash of ideas between the intractable representatives of different trends of thought. In the field of creative activity proper, modernist trends were also emerging alongside the movement towards realist literature—critical impressionism, expressionism in the theatre and visual arts, surrealism in poetry—bringing with them significant innovations in expression. The principal theorist in the modernization of culture was the critic Eugen Lovinescu (1881–1943), an outstanding figure who, through his literary circle and his review *Sburătorul*,[1] discovered new talent and fostered its development. But the progressive intelligentsia of the time was expressing its views in other publications, such as *Contemporanul* (The Contemporary) (1921), *Cuvîntul* (The Word) (1924), *Cultura Proletară* (Proletarian Culture) (1926), *Bluze Albastre* (Blue Blouses) (1932) and *Era Nouă* (New Era) (1936).

The triumph of the anti-Fascist uprising of 23 August 1944 marked the beginning of a new era in Romanian history, an era of far-reaching economic, social, political and also cultural changes. The most progressive traditions in Romanian and universal culture began to be stressed at this time, and for the first time arrangements were made for systematic action to discover talent in every domain and to help it find expression.

The setting up of the democratic government on 6 March 1945; the agrarian reform of 25 March of the same year; the abolition of the monarchy

1. Literally, 'he who flies in the air'; figuratively, 'he who flies towards other spheres, other horizons'. The word also denotes a character in Romanian poetry and fairy-tales, a nocturnal genie who lies in wait for girls, kisses them and makes them lovesick.

and the proclamation of the republic on 30 December 1947; the national-
ization of the principal means of production on 11 June 1948; the implementation in December 1948 of the plan designed to bring about the socialist
transformation of agriculture, the ninth and tenth congresses of the
Romanian Communist Party—all these steps have had a profound effect
on the Romanian people. Alongside these economic and social transfor-
mations, immense changes took place in cultural matters. Education was
reformed so as to meet the needs of modern society, and culture was
directed towards the needs of the people, so that it was able to play an
important role in the establishment of the new social and political régime.

The Romanian people's desire to preserve and cultivate its identity is
an important feature of its spiritual and cultural history. As far back as
the second half of the nineteenth century, systematic study of the country's
past was begun, preparations were made for the publication of vitally
important material concerning its existence and continuity, research into
the evolution of the Romanian language over the centuries was undertaken,
and collections of works from the wealth of its folk literature were published,
eliciting Henri Focillon's comment that, unlike others, 'there is nothing
of the archaeological survivor about it, or rather, it does not survive—it
lives'.

One of the main aims of State cultural policy at present is to enhance
the value of the nation's cultural heritage. Throughout the centuries individuals have produced works that were in the main currents of European
culture—classicism, pre-romanticism, critical realism, symbolism and mod-
ernism—in short, all the literary and artistic movements which have
marked the evolution of other cultures; in Romania, however, these have
assumed an original and sometimes syncretic form, and have been ahead
of their time. This forceful forward movement was particularly marked
from the second half of the nineteenth century onwards, a period when
outstanding figures emerged: Vasile Alecsandri (1819–90), the poet of
the union of principalities and national independence; Mihai Eminescu
(1850–89), the last of the great romantics in universal literature; Ion Creangă
(1837–89), the Homer or the Rabelais of the Romanians, as he has been
termed; and Ion Luca Caragiale (1852–1912), unquestionably the forerunner
of Eugène Ionesco. After them came the Pleiad of great writers of the period
between the two wars—Mihai Sadoveanu (1880–1961), Liviu Rebreanu
(1885–1944), Tudor Arghezi (1880–1967), Camil Petrescu (1894–1957), Lucian
Blaga (1895–1961) and Ion Barbu (1895–1961). Some of the authors of
this period—Panait Istrati, Elena Văcăresco, B. Fundoianu, Ilarie Voronca,
Tristan Tzara, Marthe Ribesco and Eugène Ionesco—have won their
place in the wider context of European literature. In the other arts,
mention should be made of the painters Nicolae Grigorescu (1838–1907),
who depicted scenes from everyday life and landscapes, Stefan Luchian
(1868–1916) and Ion Tuculescu (1910–62), both great masters of colour, the
musician Georges Enesco (1881–1955) whose magnificent rhapsodies are so

familiar to us, the sculptor Constantin Brâncuși (1876–1957), with his severely simple shapes, and many other creative artists who have gained world fame.

All these artists have achieved world-wide renown through Romanian culture. This being so, it is natural that the problem of the relationship between tradition and innovation, between the assimilation of foreign influence and the preservation of the indigenous basis should have assumed vital importance. The specialist in aesthetics, Tudor Vianu (1897–1964), points out that the evolution of modern Romanian culture has been characterized by a process of the reasoned adaptation of cultural forms to the need arising from development in social life:[1]

All our great thinkers have given consideration to this problem. Even more important is the appearance, within the context of Romanian society, of a type of intellectual whose counterpart is not readily found in other cultures—a cultured person whose knowledge is not restricted to one scientific subject, but who is concerned with all aspects of culture, and believes that he has a responsibility for helping to direct our civilization. . . . This definition applies to many distinguished figures in recent Romanian literature and thought.

Most significant of all is the fact that guidelines constituting a general cultural programme were laid down in Romania as far back as the first half of the nineteenth century, when the historian and thinker Mihail Kogălniceanu (1817–91) referred, in the preface to the review *Dacia Literară* (Literature in Dacia) (1840), to the need for a balance to be maintained between internal and foreign sources. Similar ideas are also to be found in the work of other intellectuals: poets such as Vasile Alecsandri, Mihai Eminescu, Tudor Arghezi and Lucian Blaga; theorists and philosophers such as Nicolae Bălcescu (1819–52), Titu Maiorescu (1840–1917), Constantin Dobrogeanu-Gherea (1855–1920), C. Rădulescu-Motru (1868–1957) and N. Bagdasar (1898–1971); artists such as Constantin Brâncuși and Georges Enesco; mathematicians such as Spiru-Haret (1851–1912), Grigore C. Moisil (1906–73); speleologists such as Emile Racovitza (1868–1947); and linguists such as Bogdan-Petriceicu Hașdeu (1838–1907), Ovid Densușianu (1873–1938), Sextil Puscariu (1877–1948), and so on.

This tradition lives on today in the cultural policy of the Romanian State. The desire to give expression to the cultural needs of society, to strike a balance between tradition and innovation and to co-ordinate within a single national structure the different aspects of the evolution of contemporary culture is one of the important factors in Romanian cultural policy today.

1. Tudor Vianu, *Filosofia Culturii*, 2nd ed., p. 287–8, Bucharest, 1945.

The words of President Nicolae Ceauşescu are revealing in this connexion:[1]

. . . we wish the Romanian people to be able to enjoy the best that thought, art and literature—past and present—have produced in any part of the world; we want to import literary and artistic productions, films and plays which are morally uplifting and conducive to the progress of our people, and which help to inculcate of spirit of humanism and mutual friendship. But it is the duty of society to take certain measures to prevent the entry into our country, alongside the good and the praiseworthy, of so-called works of art of doubtful content—books, films and plays in which crime, racism and brutality are condoned and which can poison the spirit and pollute the mind.

The cultural policy of the Romanian State is in keeping with the underlying quality of remarkable flexibility and the astonishing capacity for assimilation which have always been features of the Romanian people, making them receptive to a great variety of external influences, while remaining true to themselves and placing at the disposal of other peoples all that is best and most representative in their own experience. In this sense much can be learnt from our history. It has given birth to a kind of patriotism which, although unyielding, is essentially opposed to chauvinism and intolerance. The spirit of calm deliberation and understanding, the submission of instinct to reason, which are reflected throughout the whole of Romanian culture, explain why the Romanian people are on such good terms with the national groups living amongst them, and why they have always had such good relations with other peoples, whether neighbouring or remote.

This was the extremely rich soil on which Romanian socialist culture developed after the liberation from the Fascist yoke and the assumption by the Romanian nation of its place among the countries engaged in the construction of socialism. In our country, the exploitation of man by man has been abolished for all time, illiteracy has been eliminated, and the foundations have been laid for the wide dissemination of culture among the people and for the increasing participation of the people in creative cultural activity. The problems of national groups have been solved in a Marxist spirit, and harmonious co-operation has been established between the Romanian people and the national groups living among them—Hungarians, Germans, Serbs, etc. A compulsory ten-year educational system has been set up, which has given young people much wider access to the highest

1. Nicolae Ceausescu, 'Statement on the Programme of the Romanian Communist Party with a View to Improving Ideological Action and Raising the General Level of the Education of the Public at Large, Thus Establishing Relations in our Society Based on the Principles of Socialist and Communist Ethics and Justice', *Plenary Meeting of the Central Committee of the Romanian Communist Party, 3–5 November 1971*, p. 73, Bucharest, Political Publishing House.

cultural values. There has also been a marked increase in the number of students and the number of higher educational institutions. The whole country, one might say, has become a vast school. Table 1 shows how education developed in Romania in 1938/39—regarded as the most important year for Romanian development before the liberation—and in 1972/73.

TABLE 1   Development of education

Type of education	Number of pupils and students	
	1938/39	1972/73
Primary education, general secondary and specialized secondary education	1,604,481	3,220,074
Education in the arts	—	26,211
Vocational and technical training, post-secondary specialized courses and teacher training	59,533	269,752
Higher education	26,489	143,985
TOTAL	1,690,503	3,660,022

TABLE 2   Development of cultural establishments

	1938	1973
Theatres and musical establishments	18	145
Audience (in millions)	1.6	12.5
Cinemas	338	6,170
Audience (in millions)	41.4	177
Cultural centres and institutes	3,467	8,006
Amateur groups in cultural centres and institutes	3,500	22,303
Publishing		
Total number of titles	2,300	4,200
Original works	1,900	3,580
Translations	400	620
Total number of copies published (in millions)	8	72.2
Original works	6.5	56.2
Translations	1.5	16
Public libraries	3,100	7,939
Volumes (in millions)	1.1	50
Number of newspapers, magazines and periodicals published annually (in millions)	650	1,477
Museums	83	331
Visitors (in thousands)	875	11,439
Radio licences (in thousands)	252	3,077
Television licences (in thousands)	—	2,145

In addition, the State has permanently improved the material and legal conditions through which the creative spirit can find increasingly full expression; it has increased the number of theatres and musical establishments, cinemas, cultural centres and institutes, clubs, amateur groups, public libraries, publishing houses, reviews, newspapers and museums. Table 2 will give the reader some idea of the development of cultural establishments and activities between 1938 and 1973.

The principles of cultural policy

Within the context of the construction of socialism, long-term political and ideological action, the provision of socialist education and the constant improvement of the cultural standards of the public are real needs and essential factors in the process of establishing the new society. For this reason the Communist Party and the State, while concerned with the development and improvement of the means of production so as to provide the people with an abundance of material goods, attach special importance to the task of educating a new type of man and making him politically and morally conscious, and are doing everything possible to create an atmosphere which will encourage a variety of intellectual activities and the advancement of education, culture, art and literature, so that all the creative energies of the people may have a chance to come to fruition.

Romania today has entered a new phase in the evolution of socialist society a phase in which ideological problems acquire special importance. In order to apply in a creative way the great Marxist-Leninist principles proclaimed at the tenth Congress of the Romanian Communist Party in 1969, the enlarged plenary session of the central committee of the Romanian Communist Party, which was held from 3 to 5 November 1971, adopted a vast programme designed to improve ideological action, raise the general level of knowledge and of the socialist education of the people, and consolidate social relations based on socialist ethics and justice. The proceedings of this plenary session are a document of great value as regards theory, and contain detailed information about the tasks that must be undertaken in order to develop a democratic culture and help the people in their struggle for the achievement of their humanitarian ideals. In the light of this programme, which has been enthusiastically endorsed by all the people, it is even more evident that we must build up a culture whose main purpose will be to produce a richly endowed and well-balanced personality, able to contribute, actively and consciously, to the progress of socialist society

This cultural policy is the expression of the great importance attached by the State to the dissemination of culture among the people at large and to the provision of conditions whereby they can have access to all forms of culture. Culture is present everywhere; it is no longer the prerogative of an élite, but the property of the people as a whole. We believe that a modern State cannot be really free unless it takes concerted action to enable the people to attain a higher education level and, at the same time, to gain awareness of their social and moral responsibilities. In Marxist ideology, a human being is not a mere part of the production process—he is a spiritual entity who seeks constant enrichment, and who should enjoy all of the values that the socialist system can offer him. The supreme aim of our cultural policy, therefore, is the multiform development of the human personality. It is based on a deep-seated confidence in man and in his ability to improve himself. Furthermore, this new humanism corresponds to the present historical stage in the evolution of the Romanian people, to its social ideal and its conception of life. At the same time—and as a result of this—our cultural policy is inspired by the most authentic cultural values of our past, in accordance with the Marxist-Leninist principle of the enhancement of the literary heritage; nothing of merit that the past has produced escapes our notice. In this way the present joins forces with the progressive elements of the past in the effort to build a new culture. But socialist culture, while putting the best traditions of the past to good use, endeavours to be innovatory and constructive. It is receptive to modern innovations which take account of the problems of contemporary man and the life of Romanian society.

The activities to be carried out in culture and the arts constantly lead to new problems, which require solutions consonant with the needs of our continually evolving society. This is the basic idea behind Romanian cultural policy and the character of socialist art, whose purpose is to present reality in all its variety and complexity. Neither idealism nor nihilism is compatible with the essence of realist art.

Genuine creativity grasps the contradictions of existence, while stressing —and this is its most important aspect—the positive and innovatory character of development.

A spirit of constructive criticism is an essential attribute of our socialist culture. The development of culture and art in Romania is planned so that they are in the vanguard of scientific conceptions concerning the world, society, thought and, therefore, adopt a critical attitude towards anything anachronistic.

Our constant concern to ensure the triumph of social equity and justice is clearly reflected in the domain of art, for relations between men and the capacity of man for self-improvement have always been an inexhaustible source of inspiration and the very substance of genuine works of art, and they are even more so today than in the past. Nothing that concerns man is beyond the concern of our socialist culture and art.

Culture and art in Romania, while striving to express specifically national characteristics, are responsive to all that is good in universal thought, art and literature, and to everything that can contribute to humanist education from the point of view of esteem, respect and collaboration between nations.

Special importance is placed on activities aimed at educating young people in a spirit of humanism, making them love justice and work, social equity and patriotism, and fellowship with people throughout the world who are engaged in the struggle for peace, sovereignty and independence.

Our cultural policy has no place for art which is remote from life and mankind, or for creative activity that has no ultimate social purpose. The art cultivated is the expression of life, hope and man's impulse towards a better future. We seek a realist culture centred on man, with all his anguish and his material and intellectual problems. Because of this, we repeat, there is no subject, no problem, related to man that our art and our literature cannot deal with.

Literary and art critics are of special importance in the dissemination of creative works of great ethic and aesthetic value. They assess cultural works on the basis of objective and humanist scientific criteria and help the public to appreciate the intrinsic values of art and culture.

In order to ensure that cultural policy reaches an ever higher standard, the State endeavours, through research institutes and the press, to define both more clearly and more flexibly, the different concepts relating to culture and art and to re-interpret them so as to give them new dimensions.

To achieve this end, cumbersome and bureaucratic working methods which are of little real value in cultural matters have been replaced by new and more flexible methods that take the specificity of culture and its own particular function into account and are more conducive to creative activity and to the participation of the general public and specialists in cultural activities. The present system of organization tends more and more to rely on the participation of persons who have the ability, enthusiasm and devotion for this lofty task. Considerable efforts are therefore made to train efficient and well-informed organizers of cultural activities who are capable of meeting the growing demands of the modern school.

The translation into practical terms of cultural-policy principles led, first of all, to the co-ordination of all activities undertaken on the cultural front, accompanied, as is logical, by decentralization and the elimination of bureaucracy. Next working methods were improved, routine procedures and the prejudices of a few officials giving way to the creative energies of the people, inspired by their love of beauty.

It was for this purpose that the Council of Socialist Culture and Education was set up. It is an organ of the State Party, directly attached to the Romanian Communist Party Central Committee, and of the Council of Ministers. Its function is to see that the policy of the party and the State regarding socialist culture and education is applied and to direct and guide all cultural and educational activities. The establishment of this council marks a very important stage in the process of making the main body responsible for the co-ordination and direction of cultural activities as broadly democratic as possible. In establishing it, account was taken of the particularly complex nature of cultural action, which cannot be directed and guided by means of administrative methods and practices. The active participation of the most important representatives of the various categories of creative artists in the drawing up of cultural policies means that the Council of Socialist Culture and Education is being increasingly transformed into a vigorous and representative body which, basing its action on the suggestions of creative artists and those engaged in the dissemination of culture, can effectively solve all the problems involved in its many-sided and complex action.

The Council of Socialist Culture and Education, mindful of the need for decentralization and for the encouragement of initiative, and in order to give greater responsibility to the unions and organizations of creative artists, and to local party and State organs, carries out its activities in such a way that they cover the whole of the country and are supported by the competent local bodies. Its task is to broaden the cultural horizon of the people and ensure that they have access to all that is most worth while in man's creative activity in science, culture and art. The council works for the promotion of humanist ethics and for the education of all in the spirit of the progressive traditions of the people, the revolutionary principles of the working class, and fraternity between the workers—Romanian, Hungarian, German, or workers of other nationalities—who make up the great socialist family. It strives to combat retrograde ideas and does a great deal to disseminate Marxist-Leninist philosophy and to encourage a spirit of international fellowship.

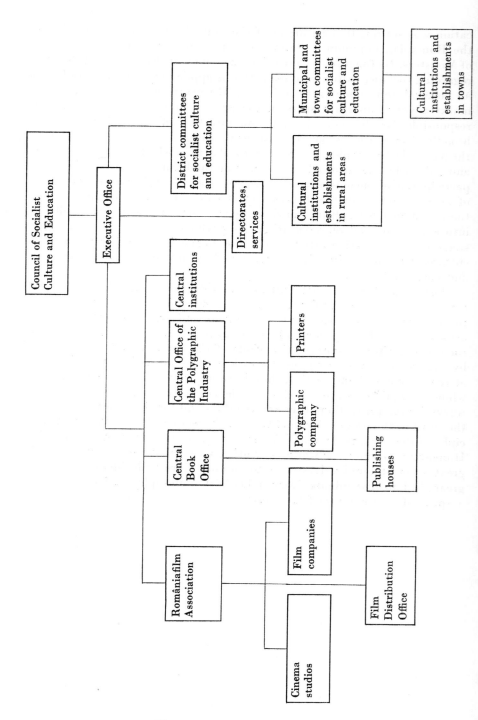

Bodies responsible for cultural and educational activities in Romania

The bodies with competence for the implementation of cultural and educational activities are as follows:

The Grand National Assembly, as the supreme State organ, exercises control over all the other State bodies.

The Grand National Assembly has standing committees which are responsible for drafting reports and for advising on draft legislation or on questions submitted to them for consideration by the president of the assembly.

The Commission for Education, Science and Culture also deals with questions that are within the competence of the Council of Socialist Culture and Education.

The State Council of the Socialist Republic of Romania, which is subordinate to the Grand National Assembly, supervises the application of the laws and decisions of the assembly and the activities of the central administrative organs and, by implication, those of the Council of Socialist Culture and Education.

The Council of Ministers directs, co-ordinates and supervises the activities of ministries, including those dealing with cultural activities.

The Council of Socialist Culture and Education, whose responsibilities and tasks are defined above, was created by Decree No. 301/1971.

The creative artists' unions (Writers' Union, Composers' Union, Artists' Union, Union of Archivists) are public, professional organizations freely established by creative artists. They receive material aid from the State and carry out their activities under the direction of the Romanian Communist Party; their purpose is to aid artists in the creation of works that support communism, works that have a rich ideological content and are of real artistic merit.

The Association of Film Workers (ACIN), the Association of Members of Theatrical and Musical Institutions (ATM), the Association of Photographic Artists (AAF) and the Librarians' Association are also publicly constituted bodies. Their task is: to contribute, at various levels, to the development of activities in their field of competence; to take part, through their representatives, in the work of the corresponding international bodies; and to disseminate information about our country and its achievements.

A particularly important role in artistic educational and cultural life is played by Romanian Radio and Television, whose programmes are broadcast to increasingly large audiences. Almost 85 per cent of broadcasting time is reserved for artistic, cultural and educational programmes.

The General Association of Trade Unions, which has responsibility for the press and the vast network of cultural centres and clubs, has organized amateur art societies with a wide variety of activities: theatre, folk dancing, ballet, choral singing, music, etc. It also possesses a very large network of libraries.

The Ministry of Education is responsible for the operation and supervision of the educational system. Since books, films and dramatic art play an important part in education, this ministry works in close co-operation with the Council of Socialist Culture and Education. A large number of school and university libraries, museums, student cultural centres and clubs come under the Ministry of Education.

The Union of Communist Youth also fulfils a very important function in the cultural domain. In almost all cultural centres and institutes the young people in the locality are responsible for the activities of amateur groups. The majority of theatre, cinema and concert audiences are young people, and they are the most frequent visitors to public libraries and museums.

The Ministry of Tourism organizes cultural and artistic events, excursions to monuments and visits to museums. Programmes of excursions are arranged for tourists, so that they can attend the main cultural and artistic events organized each year in our country (for example, the Georges Enesco International Music Festival). Since 1971, the Ministry of Tourism has been issuing a review, *Picturesque Romania*, and it is equipped with publishing facilities.

The Ministry of National Defence and the Ministry for the Interior direct cultural centres known as *Casa Armatei* (Army Houses), and are also responsible for professional groups of artists.

The Central Union of Craft Co-operatives (UCECOM) and the Central Union of Consumers' Co-operatives (CENTRO COOP) have also set up centres and clubs for cultural activities.

The people's councils in districts, towns and communes organize cultural activities for large numbers of people. In order to ensure that the cultural and educational activities of State organs and the people's associations follow the same policy, they are represented on the Council of Socialist Culture and Education.

Wooden gate, in the valley of the river Iza in the department of Maramurech, an original ethnographic zone situated in the north-west of Romania.

The town of Piatra Neamţ, 'Pearl of Moldavia'. ——→

Masa Tacerii (the 'Table of Silence'), a work of Constantin Brâncusi at Tûgu Jiu.

Amateur folk dance in a factory club (Victoria chemical factories in the Brașov district).

Books

Although the development of the various mass communication media has been as spectacular in Romania as elsewhere, books are still in the forefront because of their exceptional power of attraction, their traditional prestige and their educational value.

Several generations of creative writers have furthered the development of culture and art in line with the principles of socialist humanism. The principal ones are the novelist and short-story writer Mihail Sadoveanu, the famous poet Tudor Arghezi, to whom we owe the great philosophical poem *Song to Man* and the epic *1907*, dealing with the peasant revolt, the poet and philosopher Lucian Blaga and the writers A. Philippide and Geo Bogza.

As regards criticism, the history of literature and essays, the works of noteworthy figures such as Mihai Ralea, George Călinescu, Tudor Vianu, Perpessicius, Serban Cioculescu, Vladimir Străinu, A. Dima and Liviu Russu show that they fully support the new historical realities.

Writers who began their careers before the Second World War are now established authors and are producing masterpieces: in addition to the novelist and poet Zaharia Stancu, president of the Writers' Union, author of the novel *Barefoot*, which has already been translated into twenty-four languages, mention should be made of the profoundly original poets: Eugen Jebeleanu, Maria Banuș, Virgil Teodorescu, Geo Dumitrescu and Emil Giurgiuca; some of these were originally partisans of *avant-garde* ideas and surrealism, but held left-wing political views.

The post-liberation years saw the emergence of a great number of writers who have established a bridge between the traditions of classical Romanian literature and contemporary writing: Eugen Barbu, Marin Preda, Titus Popovici, Laurențiu Fulga, Suto Andras, Fănus Neagu, Dumitru Popescu, A. E. Baconski, Nina Cassian, Ion Brad, Mihu Dragomir, Vasile Niculescu, Alexandru Andrițoiu, Aurel Rău and, in the theatre, Horia Lovinescu, Paul Everac, Aurel Baranga, Alexandru Mirodan, Vasile Rebreanu, M. R. Iacoban and Corneliu Leu.

Much outstanding lyric poetry was written in the sixties. Nicolae Labis was symbolic of the poetry of that time, but, alongside this meteoric figure who died so prematurely, there are other eminent names such as Nichita Stănescu, Gheorghe Tomozei, Ion Alexandru, Ana Blandiana, Ion Gheorghe, Dumitru M. Ion, Adrian Păunescu, Marin Sorescu, and prose writers such as D. R. Popescu and A. Ivasiuc.

During the last twenty-five years great progress has been made in Romania in publishing activities, which not only help to implement a vast State education and training programme, but also, ultimately, are the outward expression of the country's culture. The considerable increase in the reading public and the raising of the level of their knowledge has led to the diversification of publishing activities, and also means that special care is taken with regard to the ideological content, the humanist message, and its wide dissemination among the people. Romania has adopted Unesco's slogan 'Books for All'.

As can be seen from the bibliography of published works, the aims of publishing policy are as follows: to facilitate the publication of original works, publicize the results of research in every domain and ensure that the publishing programme meets the increasingly varied reading and study needs of the modern reading public; to reveal the wealth of the Romanian scientific heritage; to stimulate literary, artistic and scientific creation among writers and scholars in the national groups living in Romania; to publish translations of great works and scientific studies that have won world-wide repute; to publish technical manuals and books for the further education and retraining of specialists, so as to enable them to meet the requirements of national economic development; to encourage the production of popular science works; to meet the demands of every category of reader and improve the dissemination of information by publishing 'series' and 'collections'; to improve the appearance of books; and to disseminate Romanian culture and scientific knowledge in other countries.

As we have already stressed, the diversity and wealth of creative activities and research have led to the adoption of measures designed to give publishing houses the means of keeping up with the pace of economic and cultural development.

New publishing houses have been set up in Bucharest and in the main university centres in the country (Jassy, Cluj, Timișoara, Craiova) and the most important newspapers—*Scînteia*, *Scînteia Tineretului*, *Elöre*, *Neuer Weg*—are embarking on publishing activities.

Authors in every category desiring to have their works published at their own expense can apply to Editions Litera. There are twenty-four publishing houses in Romania, in addition to publishing offices attached to ministries, research institutes, cultural establishments, newspapers, etc.

The present rate of development in publishing is the mark of a vigorous culture, in which the book is no longer the prerogative of a minority—it is the mental food of a very large number of readers. The number of titles, of course, demonstrates the wide variety of the subjects and themes covered and the capacity for original creation, or of assimilation, through translation, of universal values, but the number of copies published shows the extent of book distribution. The number of copies published each year by Romanian publishing houses is steadily increasing. Whereas during the years 1944–48 the average annual number of titles published did not exceed 1,400 and the number of copies published, 3.3 million, these figures rose between 1961 and 1966 to an average of over 3,000 titles per annum, with a total of some 6 million copies. The figures for the period 1966–73 provide even more striking evidence of the vigorous pace of book development: 3,880 titles were published annually, a total of 7 million copies. Between 1944 and 1973 over 140,000 titles were published, the number of copies amounting to almost 1,592 million. In 1970, the final year of the last five-year plan, four books per inhabitant were published, which means that Romania was among the leading countries in book production.

Between 1961 and 1973 over 45,000 titles appeared, and the over-all production was 862 million copies. In 1973 4,200 titles were issued in the publishing trade alone, a total of over 72 million copies (some 13 million more than in 1970), and this does not include production outside the trade.

Social and political literature occupies an important place; during the years 1966–73, 1,876 titles were published with 40,418,000 copies. In 1973 alone this type of literature accounted for 285 titles and over 4 million copies. The publication of works on history, philosophy, sociology and logic has also been marked by rapid expansion in recent years. A very important aspect of publishing activities is the publication of works dealing with contemporary history.

Practical and theoretical works on the natural sciences, technology and agriculture and medicine are published, representing Romania's contribution to the development of world science, and books designed to assist workers in the various branches of industry to qualify for more highly specialized posts, improve their knowledge and keep abreast of the latest developments in their particular fields.

The most important reference works are dictionaries and books dealing with the history of the various sciences. In the period 1949–73, 17,000 textbooks, university courses and teaching manuals (some 46 million copies in all) were printed for the use of schoolchildren, students and teachers. Comparison of these figures with those for the year 1973 alone (954 titles and 26,818,000 copies) shows the growing importance of reference works.

The production of literary works proper is increasing considerably from year to year. Between 1949 and 1973 19,288 titles (some 457 million copies) were published. Measures such as the reorganization of the publishing system in 1969, the diversification of publishing houses and the setting up of specialized ones have resulted in an increase in the number and variety of publications. Over 1,300 literary works were published in 1970, and over 28 million copies were printed. In 1973 the number of titles rose to 1,444. Contemporary literature makes considerable progress from year to year. In 1970, the first year of activity of the newly established publishing houses, 537 books were published—prose, poetry, plays, literary history and theory—the total number of copies produced amounting to 4 million.

As part of a long-term plan, action has been taken to make people more aware of Romania's literary heritage by the systematic publication of collections, accompanied by critical notes, or of separate editions of different types.

Books for children and young people have met with considerable success;

not only have the numbers published increased but, most important of all, the range of subjects has been extended, and more stress is placed on books providing information and ethical training and on the application of new and more appropriate methods of graphic and artistic layout. In 1973 the specialized publishing firms Albatros and Ion Creanga alone published 311 titles, over 9,273,000 copies.

In 1974 priority is to be given to contemporary literature; over 73 per cent of the works to be published have been produced by writers in this century. At the same time the number of reprints will be considerably reduced; they will account for barely 2.5 per cent of titles, compared with 17 per cent in 1973.

During the period 1944–73 Romanian publishing houses translated and published some 15,000 titles (over 246 million copies) of works of all kinds from over 70 foreign languages.

The 1974 plans of publishing houses responsible for the publication of translations have been rationalized as compared with those of 1973; they include the most typical works of a greater number of contemporary writers. Care will be taken to ensure that no works are published except those that meet our ideological and artistic requirements.

Apart from the criterion of merit, the choice of works from universal literature has been governed by the importance attached to creative works of a progressive kind published in any part of the world. In order to give more balanced representation to all geographical regions, publication plans for 1974 include works from Arab, African, Scandinavian, Asian and Latin American literature.

Special attention is given to art books. Between 1960 and 1969 1,794 titles of such books were published. In 1970 116 works on the visual arts in Romania and the world in general were published (1,103,000 copies) and in 1971 over 187 titles (804,000 copies). The figures speak for themselves.

The efforts made by the Romanian State to stimulate and give prominence to the culture of the national groups have had remarkable success in the publication of books. During the years 1966 to 1973, 4,752 titles were issued (over 26 million copies) in Hungarian, German, Serbo-Croat, Ukrainian and other languages as well. In 1973 640 titles (4,026,000 copies) in the languages of the national groups were published. In 1973, the publishing house Kriterion alone issued 166 titles—over 1 million copies.

Romanian culture is becoming more widely known in other countries. A great number of Romanian scientific works have been issued by important foreign publishers. Similarly, the most representative works of classical and contemporary literature have been translated in many countries. During the last twenty years, 1,759 works, translated into over 60 languages, have been published abroad. Romanian books translated into foreign languages and books about Romania have been printed during the last few years by 170 publishers in over 80 countries. Over 22,000 libraries, 1,500 bookshops in towns and villages, 6,700 shops and co-operatives, and some 13,000 persons who promote and distribute books in factories, institutions and villages help readers to obtain the books they require.

In 1973 twelve times as many books were sold in towns and villages as in 1952. In the five years between 1966 and 1970 alone the value of books purchased by readers was far in excess of 1,000 million lei.

Events such as 'Village Book Month', the 'Romanian Book Decade' and the 'National Book Exhibition' are organized each year in order to provide readers with information and keep them in touch with authors and publishing houses. International Book Year was given special attention, the national organizing committee planning over forty national events.

The ultimate purpose of publishing activities, of course, is to respond to the information, documentation and reading requirements of every category of reader. To meet these needs and to improve the distribution of books, publishing houses are striving to systematize the production of important collections, series or special editions, and to publish works centring round one of a few themes.

In the social sciences the following collections and series have won recognition: 'Contemporary Ideas', 'Works on Philosophy and Sociology', 'Works on Scientific Organization and Direction', 'Sociological Syntheses', 'Peoples, Cultures, Civilization' and 'Works on History'. Naturally the first place, particularly as regards the number of copies issued, is held by collections intended for the people at large. The oldest and most popular Romanian collection—'Everyone's Library'—which includes both Romanian and world literature, has had an unprecedented circulation: 55 million copies over 20 years (1950–70). The success of the 'Lyceum' series for schoolchildren, which has a fairly wide range of subjects, is confirmed each year by the growing demand for new editions. As in the case of 'Everyone's Library' and the 'Lyceum' collection, the 'Eminescou Library' was established to meet the needs of all students of Romanian literature, and it has always been respected for its high standards of selection. The 'Children's Library' series and 'My First Collection' are also designed for schoolchildren. The 'Twentieth-century Novel' series, whose purpose is to disseminate the most representative works of world literature of our day, is extremely popular.

There are also a number of collections and series dealing with literary criticism and literary history: 'Universitas', 'Times and Syntheses', 'Introduction to the Works of . . .', 'Encounters', 'Dialogue', 'History of Literature' (histories of Greek, Latin, French, Spanish, German and English literature have so far been published).

There are special collections and series for young people, which are designed to give them a good knowledge of the culture of our day: 'Famous Men', 'The Daring Ones', 'Cogito', 'Discussion for Young People', 'Remembrance of the Romanian Land', and so on.

Over twenty collections and series are published in Hungarian and German ('Horizon', 'Teka', 'Hungarian Writers in Romania', 'Romanian

Writers', 'Kriterion Series', 'Holiday Books', 'Schoolchildren's Series', etc.).

Publishing houses, the Central Book Office, and the Literary and Publishing Directorate of the Council of Socialist Culture and Education have embarked upon studies whose purpose is to determine future trends in book development and to decide what kind of literature should be promoted, what types of editions will be required, and so on.

Cultural and art publications

Cultural and art publications can do a great deal towards developing culture and stimulating creative activities. Cultural periodicals have a long-standing tradition in Romania. They have played an important part in building up the cultural life of modern Romania, closely following the major stages in the struggle for the national and social liberation of the Romanian people; the oldest of them, *Biblioteca Românească* (Romanian Library) goes back to 1821, the year of the establishment of the revolutionary movement led by Tudor Vladimirescu. The social struggles which marked the 1848 revolution strengthened their influence. For instance, the talented Ion Heliade-Rădulescu edited not only the review *Curierul Românesc* (Romanian Courier) but also *Curier de Ambe Sexe* (Courier of Both Sexes), the main purpose of which was to make the work of Romanian writers and translations of foreign works more widely known. In Moldavia, there was *Dacia Literară* (Literature in Dacia) (1840), which is associated with the name of the great statesman Mihail Kogalniceanu, and *România Literară* (Literature in Romania) (1855), edited by the famous poet Vasile Alecsandri; in Transylvania, *Foaie Pentru Minte, Inimă si Literatură* (Journal of the Mind, the Heart and Literature) was produced under the editorship of Gheorghe Barițiu. After the union in 1859 there appeared the well-known *Revista Română* (Romanian Review) (1861–63) and, in 1867, *Convorbiri Literare* (Literary Talks), both of which stated the principles of Romanian literary aesthetics formulated by Titu Miorescu, and contained poetry by Mihail Eminescu, plays by Caragiale, and articles by Creangă, Slavici and Duiliu Zamfirescu. The review *Contemporanul* (The Contemporary) (1881), directed by the critic Constantin Dobrogeanu-Gherea, was associated with the beginning of the workers' movement in Romania.

A feature of cultural publications between the wars was their great diversity, in particular *Viața Românească* (Romanian Life), directed by the literary critic Carabet Ibraileănu, *Sburătorul*, which is associated with the name of Eugen Lovinescu, and *Adevărul Literar şi Artistic* (Truth in Literature and Art), directed by George Călinescu. It should be noted that many cultural reviews of repute that are published in Romania today are the heirs of a long tradition which goes as far back—naturally with sometimes fairly long breaks—as the middle of the last century, or the beginning of the present century: *România Literară* (1855), *Familia* (The Family) (1866), *Literary Talks* (1867), *Albina* (The Bee) (1897), *Luceafărul* (The Morning Star) (1902), *Viaţa Românească* (1906), etc. Most of these reviews have from their beginning been concerned with important cultural, aesthetic and social problems of the day.

A large number of cultural reviews were founded after 1944, to cater for the growing diversification of cultural activities—for instance, the review *Secolul XX* (Twentieth Century), the purpose of which is to give Romanians a knowledge of contemporary world literature. Similarly, an increasingly important role is being played by district cultural reviews. They are increasing steadily in numbers, and they make a considerable contribution to the development of local cultural life. Their two functions—reflecting local cultural life by discovering and assisting talented young people, and participating in the cultural life of the country by spreading knowledge of the literature and art of the whole world—are successfully combined.

Twenty-seven of the cultural and art publications brought out in Romania are produced by the Council of Socialist Culture and Education, sixteen by unions of creative artists and ten by district committees of socialist culture and education. All reflect the government's desire to achieve a balanced cultural policy by stimulating literature in Romanian and in the languages of other peoples living in Romania. In addition to cultural and art publications in Romanian, there are seven cultural and literary publications in Hungarian, two in German and one in Serbian.

Cultural reviews may be broken down into the following categories: (a) cultural reviews of a general nature, which play a very important part in the dissemination of science and culture *Contemporanul, Flacăra* (The Flame), *Veac Nou* (The New Century), and district cultural reviews; (b) specialized cultural reviews: *Cinema*, on the Romanian cinema, *Indrumătorul Cultural* (A Guide to Culture), on the activities of houses of culture, cultural centres and people's universities, *Revista Muzeelor* (Museum Review), etc.; (c) reviews designed to stimulate literary and artistic creation: *România Literară, Luceafărul, Viaţa Românească, Teatru, Convorbiri Literare, Muzica, Steaua* (The Star), *Arta* (Art), etc.

Contemporary world literature occupies an equally important place in Romanian reviews, particularly in *Secolul XX* (Twentieth Century), a review which is comparable to the most modern publications of the kind throughout the world as regards the selection of works dealt with, the quality of the writing, graphic presentation and literary criticism, and which publishes, in whole or in part, the work of contemporary authors who have acquired great international popularity. But even apart from *Secolul XX*, contemporary world literature is fully covered in the reviews *Luceafărul*, *Familia*, Oradea, *România Literară*, Bucharest, *Orizont*, Timişoara, etc. In fact there is not one single important literary or cultural event of which the literary and art-loving public in Romania is not informed by cultural and art publications.

Reviews receive grants from the State. They have an important role to play in the development of all cultural activities—discovering and encouraging talent, organizing discussions on theoretical questions, and expressing the demands of public opinion as regards the promotion of culture, improvements in cultural working methods, and the development among the workers at large of a taste for the beautiful.

It should be noted that daily papers play an equally important part in spreading information about science and culture. In many districts local papers produce cultural and literary supplements which are of special interest.

There are also opportunities for the expression of cultural and artistic creative ability in the numerous student and school magazines, collections published by literary clubs and groups, etc.

PUBLICATIONS ISSUED BY THE COUNCIL OF SOCIALIST CULTURE AND EDUCATION

	Average number of copies per issue	
	1971	1973
In Romanian		
Contemporanul (The Contemporary), weekly	53,000	55,198
Tribuna (Tribune), weekly	8,200	8,353
Albina (The Bee), weekly	52,000	45,758
Flacăra (The Flame) and *Almanah Flacăra* (The 'Flame' Almanac), weekly	145,000	134,938
Veac Nou (The New Century), weekly	40,000	41,000
Teatru (Theatre), monthly	4,000	3,355
Cinema (Cinema) and *Almanah Cinema* (The 'Cinema' Almanac), monthly	196,400	166,330
Revista Muzeelor (Museum Review), monthly	3,000	2,970
Revista Bibliotecilor (Library Review), monthly	8,100	8,715
Indrumătorul Cultural (A Guide to Culture), monthly	11,900	11,587
Cărţi Noi (New Books), monthly	100,140	100,140
Urzica (The Nettle), fortnightly	145,300	143,597
Bibliografia RSR, seriile: cărţi, presă, note musicale (RSR Bibliography, series: books, press, music notes), fortnightly	2,040	3,420
Manuscriptum (Cărţi Românesti), quarterly	8,000	8,000

	Average number of copies per issue	
	1971	1973
Romanian Books (în limbile: franceză, rusă, germană, engleză) (in English, French, German and Russian), quarterly	8,000	8,000
Buletinul 'Monumente Istorice' (Historical Monuments Bulletin), quarterly	2,100	3,000
Poligrafia (Miscellany), quarterly	—	2,923

In Hungarian

A Hét, weekly	12,100	12,195
Uj Elet, fortnightly	23,000	22,556
Korunk, monthly (and Korunk Yearbook)	4,700	3,765
Művelődes, Indrumătorul Cultural (A Guide to Culture), monthly	2,900	2,731
Kőyvtari Szemle (Library Review), quarterly	880	1,100

In German

Volk und Kultur (People and Culture), monthly	1,050	1,030

In Armenian

Nor Ghiank, weekly	2,200	2,262

Publications for foreign readers

Revista Română (Romanian Review), quarterly		
In German	915	837
In English	1,170	1,130
In French	1,260	1,235
In Russian	1,400	1,408
România Azi (Romania Today), monthly		
In Russian	52,000	51,000
In German	6,600	6,495
In English	5,700	3,694
In Spanish	8,270	7,636
In French	10,000	10,584
România, monthly		
In Chinese	5,000	5,082
Literary supplement in Russian	—	2,109
Romanian literary studies—1973 (also publish studies in other widely-spoken languages)		

REVIEWS PUBLISHED BY UNIONS OF CREATIVE ARTISTS

Writers' Union

România Literară (Literature in Romania), weekly	25,000	26,000
Luceafărul (The Morning Star), weekly	9,000	9,411
Viața Românească (Romanian Life), monthly	4,000	2,888

	Average number of copies per issue	
	1971	1973
Secolul XX (Twentieth Century), monthly	11,000	11,056
Steaua (The Star), Cluj, fortnightly	3,100	2,987
Orizont (Horizon), Timişoara, weekly	1,600	5,952
Convorbiri Literare—Iaşi (Literary Talks—Jassy), fortnightly	1,700	2,607
Utunk—Cluj, weekly	10,280	10,508
Igaz Szo, Tîrgu-Mureş, monthly	2,400	2,135
Neue Literatur, monthly	2,100	3,778
Knijevn Jivot, Timişoara, half-yearly	—	1,500
Almanah U. S. (The Almanac of the Writers' Union)	45,000	45,000
Almanah Utunk	11,100	11,100

Composers' Union

Muzica (Music), monthly	2,200	2,141

Artists' Union

Arta (Art), monthly	4,000	4,000

Architects' Union

Architecture, monthly	3,200	3,391

Union of Romanian Communist Students' Associations

Amfiteatru (Amphitheatre), monthly	7,500	7,500

CULTURAL REVIEWS ISSUED BY THE DISTRICT COMMITTEES
OF SOCIALIST CULTURE AND EDUCATION

Săptămîna (The Week), Bucharest, weekly	75,000	75,000
Cronica (Topical Events), Jassy, weekly	5,000	6,396
Argeş, Piteşti, monthly	6,500	4,288
Astra, Braşov, monthly	5,200	5,002
Athenaeum, Bacau, monthly	6,000	4,208
Familia (The Family), Oradea, monthly	4,800	6,138
Ramuri (Branches), Craiova, monthly	5,500	4,866
Tomis, Constanţa, monthly	5,500	2,785
Vatra (The Home), Tîrgu-Mureş, monthly	6,800	4,509
Transilvania, Sibiu, monthly	—	5,200

Theatre

Though of relatively short duration by comparison with world drama, the history of Romanian drama bears witness to the continuing efforts of those who serve this art to put before the public examples of the most noble conduct and important problems of social life. Since the end of the war, culture has been considered as an important sector of social life, a complex system for influencing men's minds with a view to their full development. As culture is understood thus, the theatre naturally occupies an important place; special attention is paid to it, and it receives regular material and moral assistance from the State.

Romanian drama is rooted in the people's theatre as it was at the end of the eighteenth century and the beginning of the nineteenth century, a theatre which was itself the product of a long process of development of the folk art of earlier times. Puppet shows, which were always popular, are foremost among the types of entertainment enjoyed in the early days of the Romanian theatre, and which reflect its origins among the people. This form of entertainment as it developed paved the way for the appearance of the first great Romanian dramatist, Vasile Alecsandri. Bogdan Petriceicu Haşdeu, Ion Luca Caragiale, A. Davilla and Barbu Stefănescu-Delavrancea were also pioneers in this field; and dramatists in the period between the two wars included G. M. Zamfirescu, M. Sebastian, Camil Petrescu, Mihail Sorbul, Victor Eftmiu and Lucian Blaga.

However, the theatre reached its highest point in the last twenty-five years, when dramatic art, previously entirely dependent on private initiative, was established on a rational basis thanks to material support from the State. A group of outstanding writers—including Horia Lovinescu, Aurel Baranga, Paul Everac, Titus Popovici, A. Mirodan, Marin Sorescu, Dumitru Radu Popescu and Ion Băieşu—created remarkable dramatic works based on the life of the Romanian people and inspired by the loftiest kind of humanism. Alongside these authors, reference should be made to the producers Horea Popescu, Liviu Ciulei, Dinu Cernescu, Lucian Giurchescu, I. Taub, G. Harag, Ion Cojar and David Esrig and, in the puppet theatre, Margareta Niculescu and Florica Teodoru.

The figures show how much progress has been made over the last twenty-five years. Before 1945 there were no State-aided puppet theatres, whereas today shows are given by nineteen puppet theatres, with twenty-four companies (some of them divided into two groups, one speaking Romanian and the other a language spoken by one of the national groups, such as Hungarian or German). Similarly, only sixteen theatres were open permanently in Romania before the war (only a very small number of which were State aided) whereas today there is a network of forty-three establishments which are always open and are situated at appropriate places throughout the country. This rapid growth is the natural result of State cultural policy, which is aimed at meeting the cultural needs of the people at large. In addition, the State has adopted a series of measures to increase theatre audiences, thus extending the moral influence of the theatre. Moreover, theatre tickets are very reasonably priced. In towns which have no theatre plays are given all the year round in the houses of culture, tours are organized in the countryside and in workers' centres, and plays are broadcast by radio and television. Theatrical performances are also given for the national groups; out of forty-three theatres, six are reserved for plays in Hungarian, two in German and one in Yiddish.

Reference should be made here to the fourteen people's theatres which, while they are self-supporting and employ unpaid amateur companies, are nevertheless permanently open, and sometimes put on plays that are in the repertoire of professional theatres. The interest shown by Romanians in the theatre is also attested by the existence of numerous groups of amateur actors in houses of culture, factory clubs or cultural centres. Special producers' and actors' courses are organized for the members of such groups in people's art schools. The cost of establishing people's theatres or amateur companies and in training their members is naturally borne by the State.

The State makes substantial annual grants to theatres. For instance, in 1972 the grants made by the State to theatrical and musical institutions totalled some 293 million lei. Professional training for actors, producers, drama critics and readers is provided by an Institute for Higher Art Education in Bucharest and by a scenography class at the Institute of Plastic Art, also in Bucharest.

In addition there is a higher institute at Tîrgu-Mureş where instruction is given in Hungarian, and the Bucharest Institute for Higher Art Education has a class in which instruction is given in German. Exchanges with similar institutes in foreign countries give students the opportunity of learning about the theatre in other countries and also of spreading a knowledge of their own achievements beyond the Romanian frontier. Those who have completed a course in a higher theatrical institute are assigned to different localities by government boards.

Actors under contract to a specific establishment are entitled to act in other theatres, or in films or even on television, during the period of their contract, provided, of course, that their activities are not detrimental to the establishment to which they are under contract.

Producers enjoy the same freedom. Their obligations towards the theatres employing them leave them enough leisure to plan and stage shows in other theatres, either in Romania or in other countries.

An extensive 'retraining' programme gives those professionally employed in the theatre the opportunity of taking various types of post-graduate courses during temporary leave from their posts on full pay. The purpose of these courses is to enable them to continue their training and to give them information on recent successes and on methods and trends in theatre work both in Romania and elsewhere. The Council of Socialist Culture and Education finances travel costs for attendance at meetings, courses, etc., and pays the salaries of teachers, whether foreign or Romanian.

The State encourages—and provides material assistance for—the establishment by theatres of workshops for carrying out experiments in stagecraft in the widest sense of the term, i.e. the production of original works or of works representative of trends in world theatre today, or those in which new theatrical forms are explored. These workshops also serve to establish a more direct relationship with the public, whose approval often determines whether shows put on in the workshop are staged in the theatre. A valuable and permanent relationship with the public is also maintained by means of organized contacts in the summer season with schools, mass organizations, firms and institutions, and by the system of issuing season tickets for first nights, which has shown good results. As a result of all these measures the number of interested theatregoers has grown from 1,577,000 in 1938 to 12,500,000 in 1973.

For each theatre season directors, producers and readers submit proposed programmes of plays to the workers' committees, the very existence of which shows the profoundly democratic nature of theatrical activity in Romania. The programmes are then discussed and approved by the local and central State authorities. In addition to the programme for each season, theatres are continually working on their future repertoire, which is expected to show what each theatre is contributing to the theatrical life of the country.

Many plays by authors from the socialist countries are staged in Romanian theatres, from the classical authors onwards—Tolstoy, Gogol, Chekhov, Ostrovsky, Maxim Gorky, M. Kalman, M. Zsigmond, Jokay Mor, Katona Jozsef, Madach Imre, B. Nușici—up to and including contemporary dramatists such as A. Arbuzov, V. Axionov, V. Kataev, L. Kruczkorosev, Jan Otcenasek, K. Capek, Bertold Brecht, Gyarfas Miklos, Nemeth Laszlo and others.

The same criteria—the search for genuine artistic and human values and the desire to inform the Romanian public about current trends in world drama—govern the selection of western works. Classical drama is always to be seen in Romania—Greek and Latin classical writers, Shakespeare, and neo-classical and romantic authors. Famous authors such H. Pinter, J. Osborne, J. Kilty, N. St Grey, F. Durrenmatt, Max Frisch, J. Anouilh, A. Camus, E. Ionesco, P. Weiss, E. de Filippo, F. Garcia Lorca, E. O'Neill, Thornton Wilder, Tennessee Williams, A. Miller, W. Saroyan and E. Albee give the Romanian public an over-all view of contemporary western drama. Romanian theatres always make it their aim to encourage original creative work and to disseminate classical and contemporary work from every country; they put on thirty to forty first performances a year, including a score of first performances of Romanian works.

Original works written in the languages of the national groups are similarly fostered and encouraged.

The Council of Socialist Culture and Education and the Writers' Union take action to defend dramatists' material and moral rights in various ways: by purchasing their works; printing them or having them performed; holding competitions; awarding prizes; etc.

Theatrical activities are co-ordinated by the directorate of establishments for artistic entertainment and the plastic arts of the Council of Socialist Culture and Education, which is responsible for professional and ideological guidance in all sectors of culture. Working with the Association of Members of Theatrical and Musical Institutions (ATM), who are eminent artists, writers and journalists, the Council of Socialist Culture and Education organizes national and international meetings for exchanges of experience, annual discussions on developments in the art of the theatre in Romania, etc. The Romanian Agency for Artistic Impresarios (ARIA) organizes exchanges of companies under the cultural agreements that have been concluded with a large number of States.

Music

For some years now, the musical world has been active as never before. Its vigour is apparent in the vast network of musical institutions—symphony orchestras, opera houses, ballet, operetta and variety theatres, conservatoires, etc.—in the scope of the amateur movement and in the increasing frequency with which Romanian works are performed and Romanian executants appear in the great musical centres of the world.

Romanian folk music, of course, is characterized by a great variety of melodies and rhythms and by its power of expression. As a result of unfavourable historical circumstances, attempts to bring to light the richness of folk music by transcribing it remained unco-ordinated, anonymous and unimpressive. In the nineteenth century, however, social and historical conditions were favourable to the foundation of a 'national school', which sought to explore the wealth of folk music. A number of artists distinguished themselves in this sphere, including Alexandru Flechtenmacher and Eduard Caudella, Gheorghe Dima and Gavril Musicescu, George Stephanescu, Ciprian Porumbescu and others. Georges Enesco—a musician who was a composer, a virtuoso performer on the violin, a pianist and a conductor, and who worked indefatigably to stimulate musical activities in

Romania—incorporated in his work the best results of these investigations.

Between the wars musical life was more or less limited to the activities of individuals—enthusiastic but unorganized—but in recent decades exceptionally rapid progress has been made thanks to the rational policy adopted by the State. Before the war there were only two symphony orchestras in Romania, both in Bucharest, and two opera houses, one in Bucharest and one in Cluj. There are now fifteen philharmonic societies and symphony orchestras, five opera and ballet houses, four theatres with a repertoire consisting of opera, ballet and operettas, one theatre for operettas and nine variety theatres. Forty-three ensembles and groups have been founded to stimulate choral singing, folk singing and folk dancing. It should be noted that the State broadcasting company and six philharmonic societies have large choirs. All the musical institutions listed above are financed from the State budget, with an annual allocation of some 293 million lei.

Much has been done to promote the development of musical institutions and musical life; reduced rates are offered, special concerts (with very popular programmes) are held, educational concerts are organized for students and schoolchildren, and orchestral tours are arranged in the countryside and in centres where there are large numbers of workers. There are also a great number of radio and television educational programmes. Audiences in Romania today may be said to be both generous and exacting, and they have acquired the habit of frequent attendance at concerts and operas. The repertoire of musical establishments comprises the best works of Romanian composers and of composers throughout the world, both classical and modern.

Great attention is paid to new works. Each concert programme of symphonic or chamber music includes at least one Romanian work, so that some 500 to 600 new works are performed in a single season.

Carrying on a tradition in which there are many famous names, Romanian artists maintain high standards of musicianship. Soloists such as Ion Voicu, Valentin Gheorghiu, Radu Adulescu and Stefan Ruha, opera singers such as Nicolae Herlea, Elena Cernei and Ludovic Spiess, conductors such as Mircea Besarab, Iosif Conta, Ion Baciu, Mircea Cristescu, Mihai Brediceanu and Emil Simon, ballerinas such as Magdalena Popa and Ileana Iliescu, and many other artists have long since made their name on the international scene. The Madrigal choir, conducted by Marin Constantin, is highly thought of, both at home and abroad. All these categories of artists are paid members of the staffs of musical establishments. The most gifted students at institutes of musical education take part in concert seasons before completing their studies.

Future musicians are trained at three *conservatoires* (institutes of higher education) and in colleges of musical education (where, in addition to basic training in their future profession as artists, students receive the same general education as that provided in schools giving a general education).

The care taken of young musicians does not come to an end when they

39

start work. Those who are talented as soloists are helped to turn their ability to the best account. They are invited to play at concerts, take special courses under the supervision of the best teachers, receive fellowships for study abroad and are trained to perform at major international competitions. According to the latest statistics, Romania takes third place for prizes gained in international competitions.

Festivals and competitions

First on the list comes the Georges Enesco International Music Festival, which takes place in Bucharest every three years and was held for the sixth time in the autumn of 1973, providing an opportunity for talented Romanian musicians to be heard. Periodically a series of events are held in certain towns (some of which have a long-standing tradition in this field) and these towns become centres of cultural activity. Examples are Cluj with its festival the Cluj Music Lover, Timișoara (Timișoara and Music), Brașov with its chamber music festival, Sibiu (The Cibinium Festival), Tîrgu-Mureș (The Musical days of Tîrgu-Mureș), Craiova (The Maria Tanase Festival and Competition) and Mamaia (annual festival and competition of Romanian light music).

The record publishing firm Electrecord produces a large number of high-quality records. Its aims are to satisfy the tastes of the public and to meet the requirements of musical education. Electrecord also exports and imports records. The Composers' and Music Lovers' Union guides its members in their creative work, stimulates artistic activity and fosters musical life in various ways. It commissions work, makes purchases and organizes competitions to help creative musicians. The problems facing composers are regularly discussed at meetings held by the Composers' Union, in music lovers' clubs and among audiences of all kinds, for example, in firms and factories. The publishing firm of the Composers' Union publishes the best musical works and books on musicology.

Contemporary Romanian music is noteworthy not only for the amount of work produced but also for the diversity of styles. After the death of some of the brilliant representatives of the 'Enesco generation'—Mihail Jora, Paul Constantinescu, Sabin Dragoi—many outstanding personalities achieved eminence in music—Dimitrie Cuclin, Martian Negrea, Ion Dumitrescu, Theodor Grigoriu, Anatol Vieru, Wilhel Berger, Pascal Bentoiu and Tiberiu Olah.

Amateur music societies

The access of the people at large to organized forms of musical activity, such as choirs, orchestras, folk ensembles or light music groups, is rendered possible by the resources made available to them by the State and trade unions: cultural clubs and centres; the provision of musical instruments; teaching by qualified teachers; the printing and dissemination of suitable materials; the organization of amateur musical competitions and festivals; and participation by the best groups in international folk-music festivals.

In addition there is a constant interchange between the activities of professional and amateur musicians. Professional conductors and composers put their talents and ability at the disposal of certain amateur groups, and State musical institutions encourage these groups and music lovers' clubs in firms and schools; also musicians who become professionals not infrequently rise from the ranks of amateur artists.

The preservation and study of folklore are the responsibility of the Institute of Ethnography and Folklore, whose record library, the richest in south-east Europe, justifiably arouses the interest of specialists from the world over. Romanian folklore and that of the national groups are carefully classified according to scientific methods, and collections by genre and by region are made. Collections of folk music, which are an inexhaustible source of inspiration to composers, are regularly added to the repertoires of folk *ensembles* and groups, radio and television programmes and the national record archives.

One of the most characteristic features of musical life in Romania today is the active participation of Hungarian and German musicians and of musicians belonging to other national groups living in Romania in the building up of a single Romanian musical culture. Some notable composers and artists belong to these national groups. In Cluj, in addition to the Romanian Opera House, there is a state theatre on the same lines, which produces not only operas and operettas by Romanian composers of Hungarian origin but also the traditional operatic repertoire translated into Hungarian. The artistic *ensembles* of Tîrgu-Mureș and Timișoara perform new works by Hungarians, Germans and Serbs, as well as Romanian music. In addition, the members of the Council of Socialist Culture and Education, the Directorate of the Union of Composers and other musical institutions, and those connected with publishing firms and the record publishing firm Electrecord, include musicians of other nationalities such as Hungarians and Germans, as well as Romanians; radio and television broadcasts also make use of members of these other nationalities.

Films

Professional film-making activities are co-ordinated by the Româniafilm Association, a body which is responsible to the Council of Socialist Culture and Education and which deals with the production and distribution of films. Four Romanian companies make feature films, the Alexandru Sahia Studio makes newsreels, documentaries and science films, and the Animafilm Studio makes animated cartoons, filmstrips and advertising films. Between 1949 and 1973 these companies made 232 feature films, most of which were exported to more than 40 countries throughout the world. In 1973 24 full-length feature films and some 268 short films were made in Romania. The studios also undertake co-productions with foreign companies.

The films made in all the Romanian studios are essentially educational in character. Among the films which are remarkable for the originality of their ideas and the freshness of their artistic outlook, mention may be made of *Michael the Brave, The Dacians, Endless Youth, Sunday at Six, The Forest of the Hanged, The Waves of the Danube, The Stranger, Codin, The Soiree, The Power and the Truth* and the *Stone Wedding*.

The fact that for the past twenty years the price of admission to Romanian cinemas has been the lowest in the world indicates the importance attached to the cinema as a means of education.

The criterion of educational value is also applied to the production of national films and to the selection of foreign films for screening in the 615 city cinemas and 5,555 village cinemas, which are attended by some 177 million spectators annually. These cinemas also show special series of films, which attract nation-wide interest—for example, screen adaptations of famous library works, films about important historical figures or events, musical films and masterpieces of world cinema. In other words, while the cinema is used to guide the public and raise its standards of taste, it also performs a more generally instructive role. Besides a full-length feature film, each programme given at the country's 6,000 cinemas includes one or two short documentary films on educational, scientific or artistic subjects. In addition, there are more than 3,000 projectors in secondary and primary schools, and pupils can see programmes chosen from about a thousand popular science films, travelogues, films on art, medicine, health and so on.

In addition to this everyday educational work done by the cinema, mention should be made of the following special events:

The annual village film festival held over a two-month period in more than 4,000 cinemas, and accompanied by many educational activities: seminars, lectures, competitions and literary evenings. The films shown at these festivals include films specially made for agricultural tech-

nicians and films on agricultural and zootechnical innovations, which are intended to give farm workers information about their work. The annual village film festival regularly attracts 11 million spectators.
Similarly, a school film festival on themes which are chosen in advance is organized each year during the winter holidays.
The Româniafilm Association regularly carries out public opinion surveys, the results of which are analysed by its specialized services and used as guidelines for future productions.

Museums

Museums have a triple role to play in connexion with the artistic and natural heritage of the country: familiarization, preservation and presentation for educational purposes. Museological institutions are centres of intense cultural and educational activity; they carry out research and see to the protection of cultural property.

During the inter-war period, a number of eminent scholars contributed to Romanian museology, including the historians Nicolae Iorga and Vasile Pîrvan, the sociologist Dimitrie Gusti and the naturalist Grigore Antipa, but in the past three decades in particular museology has come into the foreground of the cultural life of the country. This remarkable development is based on the existence of a national heritage which is almost unparalleled elsewhere in the world.

We need only recall the magnificent sculpture and painted ceramics of the Neolithic period, such as *The Thinker* from Cernavodă, which belongs to the Hamangea culture, the painted ceramics from the Cucuteni and Gumelnița cultures, the treasures of the Thracians and the Geto-Dacians and the sculptures of the period of Roman occupation. The originality and importance of these objects are such that their significance extends beyond the frontiers of Romania; they are part of the cultural heritage of the world.

During the post-war period, existing museums such as the Village Museum and the Grigore Antipa Museum of Natural History at Bucharest were reorganized on scientific principles and enriched by new acquisitions, while a network of museums forming an integral part of the over-all system of cultural institutions was established; the museums were carefully sited so as to cover the whole country, and displayed material representative of the heritage, traditions and cultural property of each region. Among the museums thus created are the Museum of the History of the Socialist Republic of Romania, the Museum of Art and the Museum of the History of the Communist Party, as well as historical, ethnographical and folk-art museums, natural science museums, art museums and memorial museums. Similarly, a number of specialized museums, such as the open-air ethnographic museums, have been established; they include the People's Technological Museum at Dumbrava Sibiului; the Museum of Enology and Pomology at Goleşti; the Engineer Dimitrie Leonida Museum at Bucharest; the Mining Museum at Petrosani; the Gold Museum at Brad; the Navy Museum at Constanţa; the Museum of the Ancient City of Histria; the Museum of the Dacian Settlement at Sarmisegetuza; and the museums of the Putna and Sucevita Monasteries and the Monastery of Cozia. Museums at Bacău, Focşani, Turnu Severin and elsewhere display the flora and fauna of Romania.

Efforts have also been made to determine how museum work should be organized and to make research and acquisition work more systematic. Specialists are trained on the basis of rational principles and in accordance with long-term plans.

The museum network in Romania comprises the following 331 establishments: museums of art, 61; museums of history and archeology, 66; museums of natural science, 32; museums of technology, 5; memorial museums, 70; museums of ethnography and popular art, 38; general museums, 59. This list does not include the steadily increasing number of village museums.

In 1973, more than 11 million people visited museums. The annual budget for research and acquisitions at present amounts to more than 5 million lei, and is steadily increasing.

The Museum of Art of the Socialist Republic of Romania, which occupies a wing of the Palace of the Republic, has more than 80,000 exhibits; in the National Gallery of Treasures of Ancient Romanian Art, icons, fragments of frescoes, jewellery, embroidery, ceramics and wood carvings are displayed, together with exhibits from mediaeval times and the work of such national painters and sculptors as Rosenthal, Aman, Negulici, Grigorescu, Andreescu, Luchian, Paciurea, Brâncuşi, Pallady, Petrascu, Tonitza, Steriadi, Baba and Ciucourencu, to mention only a few. The Gallery of World Art includes works from various European schools, with masterpieces by Rembrandt, El Greco, Titian and others, together with a collection of far-eastern *objets d'art*, including some magnificent Chinese jade. Exhibitions of drawings, engravings, etc., are regularly held in the graphic arts room.

Another establishment of national importance is the Museum of the History of the Socialist Republic of Romania, which, although founded more recently, possesses a very large collection. It displays archaeological discoveries representative of the earliest Romanian culture, objects from the Daco-Roman civilization, remains of the Greek civilization on the shores of the Black Sea and vestiges of other ancient civilizations discovered on

44

Romanian soil. The political, social and intellectual history of the feudal and modern periods is shown so that the struggle of the Romanian people for freedom, social justice and national unity is made clear. There are many examples of the period of socialist construction in Romania. The museum also has a well-stocked section devoted to antique and mediaeval precious stones, a collection of jewels and other valuable objects and a numismatics room.

The Museum of the History of the Communist Party and of the Revolutionary and Democratic Movement gives an over-all view of the social and political movements of modern Romania.

The Village Museum is world-famous, and the pride of the Romanian capital. It extends over an area of more than 9 hectares, and includes more than 300 peasant buildings grouped together in 66 different units, each of which forms a rural settlement. The authenticity and the outstanding artistic value of these buildings make the museum a treasure-house of the people's architecture and art; it is of European importance in that it brings together these remains of an agrarian civilization which once prevailed throughout the continent, but which today has almost disappeared.

A similar museum, but one which illustrates another aspect of popular culture is the People's Technological Museum at Dumbrava Sibiului. This open-air display of buildings and equipment shows the ingenuity and inventiveness of craftsmen throughout the historical development of the country. The people's technological museum forms part of the Brukenthal Museum at Sibiu, which, in addition to the art gallery that gave it its name, also includes a gallery of national art, a museum of south Transylvanian folk art and a museum of archaeology and history.

Historical and archaeological museums are probably the most important parts of Romania's museum network. They include large archaeological museums (at Constanța, Deva, Piatra-Neamț and Drobeta-Turnu Severin) whose development is due not only to the wealth of excavated remains but also to a long tradition of research, as well as historical museums which portray the evolution of the country from the earliest times up to the period of socialist construction (the Historical Museum at Oradea, the Transylvanian Historical Museum at Cluj, the Moldavian Historical Museum at Jassy and the Historical Museum at Brașov). Other museums such as the Museum of Mediaeval Moldavian Civilization at Suceava, the Museum of the Union of 1859 at Jassy and the Museum of the Union of 1918 at Alba Iulia, are devoted to specific aspects of mediaeval or modern history.

There are also excellent ethnographical museums, the most remarkable being the open-air museums, which differ from region to region. Those at Craiova, Suceava, Satu Mare, Vîlcea, Timișoara and Baia Mare contain masterpieces of architecture and art produced by the people, and each highlights the specific characteristics of the peoples living in the region.

In view of the changes which industrialization is bringing to the countryside, the Romanian State has adopted a policy for safeguarding and preserving examples of traditional craftsmanship, either by preserving ancient dwellings *in situ* or by bringing specimens together in museum buildings or in the open air.

The most remarkable progress made in the field of museology has been in art museums. A network which was relatively balanced geographically having been set up, the collections were reorganized and representative museums, such as the Museum of Art at Bucharest, came into being. Following a systematic acquisitions policy, these museums built up an excellent collection of Romanian art, so that they are of the greatest educational importance. After this, specialized museums—such as the Museum of Modern Art at Galați, the Museum of Decorative Art at Buzău and the Museum of Primitive Art at Pitești—and with small museums containing individual collections devoted to a single person, a specific period or a particular social and cultural *milieu* were added to the network.

In the natural sciences, there are two major tasks: to show the world of nature in all its beauty and variety; and to contribute to the education of the public. Here, perhaps the most interesting achievement is the construction of the museum complex at Constanța, which includes a dolphin pool, a pool for seals, a planetarium, an observatory for the public and a scale model of a delta. An aquarium and a park are to be added in the future.

The Museum of Romanian Literature is remarkable in that it gives an extremely detailed picture of the nation's literature from its beginnings. In addition, a number of smaller museums are devoted to the life and work of famous men of letters: the Museum of Literature at Jassy, the Mihai Sadoveanu Museum at Vînători (district of Neamț), the Mihai Eminescu Museum at Ipotești (district of Suceava), the Tudor Arghezi Museum at Bucharest, the Ion Creangă Museum at Neamț, the Octavian Goga Museum at Ciucea near Cluj, the Ady Endre Museum at Oradea, and others.

One of the main objectives of museums policy is to make these institutions play a real part in patriotic, civic, aesthetic and scientific education, and temporary exhibitions, conferences and symposia are organized for this purpose. The State encourages the production of slides, films and television programmes, and all the different educational techniques are used—demonstrations, audio-visual aids, classes for schoolchildren and students in the museums themselves, etc.

In future, so that the cultural heritage may be exploited to the fullest possible extent, all that makes up the cultural heritage, including both museum collections and cultural property *in situ*, is to be centralized, and steps will be taken to organize the work more efficiently so as to take account of both subject-matter and the comparative urgency of research, on the basis of long-term plans.

The establishment of a great number of local museums reflects the increasing importance of museums as vehicles for the expression of community consciousness, and is a sign of the remarkable vigour and maturity acquired by the people as a result of the policies of the Communist Party of Romania.

Historic monuments

The preservation and presentation of the historic monuments of the Socialist Republic of Romania are an integral part of the cultural policy of the State, and monuments are regarded as providing outstanding evidence of the history of the people's creativity. Romania has a great variety of monuments, owing to various historical, social, political and geographical factors, and ancient Romanian art is a unique blend of Western trends in art and Byzantine tradition. The originality and expressive power of Romanian art have been recognized and stressed by such world-famous scholars as Charles Diehl, Henri Focillon, Puig y Gadafalch, Andre Grabar, Viktor Lazarev and many others, but above all by the national school of historians led by Nicolae Iorga and G. Balș.

The most ancient monuments discovered on Romanian territory are probably the architectural complexes of Dacian cities—Sarmisegetuza, Costești and Piatra Roșie—south of the Carpathians, whose construction techniques and conception are unique in European civilization.

The salient point about the later, Roman monuments of Transylvania (Ulpia Trajana, Porolissum, Apulum), Oltenia (Drobeta, Romula) and Dobruja (Adamclissi, Histria) is their diversity, which is due to their situation at the meeting-point of two major ancient civilizations—those centred in the eastern Mediterranean and in central Europe. This syncretism reveals both the importance of Roman civilization of the Carpatho-Danubian region in Greco-Roman culture and its originality; it is indeed a storehouse of forms and ideas in the sphere of the plastic arts, which subsequent centuries have inherited.

We need only recall the exceptional flowering of the arts during the fourteenth century, under the first rulers of the Basarab dynasty, when a number of impressive monuments with admirable wall-paintings were erected (Curtea de Argeș, Cozia). In Moldavia during the brilliant reign of Stefan cel Mare (1457–1504), a specifically Moldavian style emerged, combining elements of Byzantine and Gothic architecture (Pătrauți, Botoșani, Neamț), and a vigorous school of painting also came into being at this time. Developing the heritage left by this school, the sixteenth century produced the splendid buildings with paintings on the outside walls which have given ancient Romanian art its world-wide reputation. The paintings on the monasteries of Humor, Vatra Moldoviței, Arbore, Voroneț and Sucevița—to name only the best-known examples—are astonishing not only because of their intrinsic beauty but also because of their state of preservation, despite rain, wind and the severe winters of the region. It is because they are so valuable that these paintings are being given close attention by Unesco, and that they are to be protected and restored. Mention should also be made of the monuments erected during the reigns of Neagoe Basarab (1512–20) and Constantin Brâncoveanu (1688–1714), the sturdy peasant settlements of Transylvania and—most important of all—the wooden churches of Maramureș, which Iosef Strzgowski placed among the world's masterpieces of wooden architecture. While they form part of the European artistic heritage as a whole, these monuments are a testimony to the originality of the Romanian people and an important factor in the national consciousness.

Each year the monuments of Romania attract a great number of foreign tourists, and for this reason studies are being made of the possibility of arranging special tours to enable visitors from all over the world to acquaint themselves directly with these monuments, which are of universal interest.

The supervision of all activities connected with the protection, conservation and restoration of historic monuments is entrusted by various decrees and regulations to the Directorate of Historic and Artistic Monuments, which is itself placed under the authority of the Council of Socialist Culture and Education. The people's councils of the locality in which the monuments are situated are responsible for carrying out these activities. The Directorate of Historic and Artistic Monuments comprises the following sections:

The Advisory Management and Supervisory Section. This section keeps a record of all work carried out on historic monuments, in the protected areas surrounding them and in areas listed as centres of historical interest. In listed and protected areas, the approval of the Directorate of Historic and Artistic Monuments must be obtained before undertaking any activity involving demolition or construction, roadworks, artificial lighting, repairs of façades and roofs, the planting of trees, etc. The boundaries of protected areas are fixed in accordance with the advice of the Technical and Scientific Council for Historic Monuments and in agreement with the people's councils concerned.

The section advises local authorities as to arrangements for the local protection of monuments, the allocation of sums earmarked for restoration in the district budget, etc. It provides technical assistance in the preparation and execution of restoration projects, supervises the local protection of monuments and makes proposals for the allocation of emergency restoration funds provided by the Directorate of Historic and Artistic Monuments, taking account of the degree of damage in each case.

All these activities are carried out with the assistance of the local authorities and more specifically the committees for socialist culture and education and the directorates of systematization, architecture and supervision in each district; each directorate includes among its members a person responsible for the local protection of monuments. The Directorate of Historic and Artistic Monuments provides advice concerning the work to be carried out, after examining proposals submitted by the district concerned or by the directorate of systematization.

The Studies and Research Section. This section is responsible for keeping the inventory of historic monuments up to date as research progresses. In 1955 the government approved the first list of 4,327 monuments. A new list, now being prepared, contains some 5,800 monuments and 19 protected areas of mediaeval architecture. Age, historical value and artistic value are the criteria for the inclusion of a monument in this list. Most, but not all, of the monuments date from before 1850; great attention is paid to nineteenth-century folk architecture and industrial buildings, and to buildings which date from the turn of the century.

A detailed inventory of examples of civic architecture of the nineteenth century and the first half of the twentieth century, including modern buildings, is also to be compiled. Historic monuments are not listed in order of importance, because it is felt that such classification must inevitably involve subjective judgements.

In recent years, 480 protected areas have been added to the inventory, preference being accorded to mediaeval fortified towns.

The Studies and Research Section also carries out the following tasks: (a) publication of the inventory of historic monuments, with a brief description of each (furniture excepted); (b) compilation and publication of a repertory of monuments in each administrative and territorial unit, with a full description of them and an inventory of their furniture; (c) research, prior to restoration, into the historical, artistic and archaeological features of monuments, study of new information brought to light during their restoration, and scientific presentation of completed restoration work. Priority in research activities is accorded to restoration projects planned by the Directorate of Historic and Artistic Monuments, but support is also provided for the most important research undertakings at the local level.

The Projects and Implementation Section. This section is responsible for the restoration of the most important of the nation's monuments, selected according to their historical and artistic value, the degree of urgency of the work to be carried out and their importance as tourist attractions. The Directorate of Historic and Artistic Monuments provides for some forty restoration projects to be undertaken each year, the duration of the work varying from case to case. Among the most important projects undertaken by the directorate, mention should be made of the restoration of the fortresses of Neamţ and Tîrgu-Mureş, the monastery at Neamţ, the governor's residence at Tîrgovişte, the monastery at Suceviţa, the mosaics at Constanţa, the castle of Hunedoara, the monastery at Hurez, and many others.

The local protection, conservation and restoration of monuments are the responsibility of the people's councils in each district, whose committees for socialist culture and education supervise the presentation of monuments. The directorates of systematization, architecture and supervision act in an advisory and supervisory capacity and provide technical assistance in restoration work.

The annual budgets of the people's councils in each district include allocations for the conservation and restoration of the most important local monuments, or of monuments which are in an advanced state of decay. Recently, the façades of entire streets, or even of entire quarters (for example, the Curtea Veche quarter in Bucharest), have been restored. In addition to the funds provided by the Directorate of Historic and Artistic Monuments and the people's councils in each district, restoration work is financed by: (a) resources from the Department of Religious Cults for the repair of churches ranked as historical monuments; and (b) resources from the users of the buildings classified as monuments (ministries, dioceses, private owners, etc.).

It is the policy of the Directorate of Historic and Artistic Monuments to treat repairs of any kind, on whatever scale, as restoration work and to carry them out in such a way as to enhance the value of the monument concerned. To this end the State encourages the public to take an interest in the conservation and preservation of the heritage of monuments. Restoration is only one aspect of this work, which also includes publications, lectures, radio and television programmes, and so on. Local authorities and all who use the monuments participate in the work of conservation and presentation, which is conducted and co-ordinated in accordance with directives prepared by the Directorate of Historic and Artistic Monuments in consultation with the local authorities. In functional and economic terms, centres of historical interest are seen both as relics of a particular age or region, and—with in the context of urban renewal—as links with a town's historic past. In view of their unique potential for the development of tourism, priority has been accorded recently to the presentation of centres of historical interest. Efforts are being made to integrate monuments and centres of historical interest with contemporary life, by using them in ways which meet the social needs of our day. In other words, the aim is to instil new life into centres of historical interest and not merely to preserve them as relics of the past. Finally, scientific methods are used in restoration and care is taken to avoid subjectivism and improvisation in accordance with the guidelines of the Venice Charter.

The entire policy of the Socialist Republic of Romania with regard to historical monuments may be summarized as one of service to the cause of the people's culture and the patriotic and socialist education of the masses. Monuments are thought of not only as being of value in themselves but as a force that can have a real influence on people; they are carefully preserved because of all that they stand for, as tangible evidence of the nation's past.

Dissemination of knowledge and culture among the people

The aim of cultural activities in Romania is to help each citizen to keep abreast of progress in all fields of human knowledge and, more particularly, in subjects related to his work and to his political, cultural, scientific and artistic interests, to play an active and conscious part in social life, to cultivate his creative capacities and to make full use of the technical and material advantages which modern civilization places at his disposal.

Central or local bodies are responsible for the pursuit of this aim—either organs of the State, such as the Council of Socialist Culture and Education, the Ministry of Instruction and Education, the Ministry of Health, and so on, workers' organizations such as the General Association of Trade Unions, the Union of Communist Youth, the Union of Communist Students' Associations, the National Union of Agricultural Co-operatives, the Women's National Council, the unions of creative workers, scientific societies, etc. Thus, apart from the schools, there is an extensive system for the development of the means of spreading culture among the people, which are available to all citizens, irrespective of age, sex, profession, nationality or place of residence.

State activity in this sphere is increasing continually. The growth in expenditure on cultural activities between 1955 and 1973 (in millions of lei) is as follows: 1955, 6,992; 1960, 14,103; 1965, 22,361; 1970, 35,942; 1971, 38,861; 1972, 42,591; and 1973, 45,000.

It will be seen that State expenditure on culture in 1973 was double that in 1965, and amounted to more than 2,200 lei per inhabitant; to this sum should be added the financial resources made available for cultural development activities by the different workers' organizations, and the funds raised by cultural establishments themselves through their own activities.

One indication of this progress is the fact that a vast network of cultural establishments of different types has been set up, including approximately 8,000 cultural centres and houses of culture, and 22,000 amateur artists' groups.

Cultural centres,
houses of culture, clubs

The cultural centres, which occupy a key position in each commune and in most of the villages, and the houses of culture and clubs, which are to be found in every town, play a leading role in local cultural life and have gained great popularity. In 1973, for example, some 46 million citizens participated in 600,000 cultural events organized by the houses of culture and cultural centres, while attendance at village cinemas, which are part of the cultural centres, amounted to approximately 65 million.

At the same time, the organization of various circles, clubs or associations in cultural centres and houses of culture enables them to cater increasingly for minority interests and requirements ('micro-groups').

Libraries

A major contribution to the instruction and education of the people is made by libraries, which number more than 22,500 and figure prominently in the educational policy of the Romanian State. After the Second World War, a vast network of libraries was set up, comprising State public libraries (approximately 8,000), libraries of trade unions and other workers' organizations (4,807), school libraries (10,300) and the national libraries (Library of the Academy and the Central State Library).

At the end of 1973, the holdings of Romanian libraries amounted to some 124 million volumes. Between 1965 and 1973, public libraries acquired more than 30 million volumes. At the end of 1973, the number of readers in the various categories of libraries was estimated at more than 8 million, and they consulted over 81 million books. The fact that 10 per cent of the urban population and 22 per cent of the rural population have become active readers is indicative of the extent to which public libraries are geared to the various interests and requirements of modern society.

The libraries also carry out a great many educational activities, they publish catalogues and bibliographies, undertake studies of reading requirements, etc. This work is done by the 3,000 qualified librarians, specialized training in librarianship having been introduced recently.

People's universities

Various forms of adult education are available in Romania, and a variety of means are used to support it. Moreover, under recent legislation a well co-ordinated system has been introduced to provide pre-service and in-service training and retraining for managerial personnel in the economic sector and all other sectors of social life and for workers in factories and other establishments.

Of all these forms of adult education, which include lecture series or readings on the most varied topics, the work done in the villages by 'brigades' of scientists and specialists in various fields, meetings with scientific experts, the distribution of brochures and the screening of popular science films, the organization of exhibitions, the publication of 'photo-newspapers', the projection of slides, etc., the people's universities are of special importance. They are open to all who seek to improve their knowledge and, for the most part, are attached to houses of culture and cultural centres. In 1970/71 there were 302 people's universities giving 2,064 courses to a total of 120,000 students, while by 1971/72 they had developed to the point where 401 establishments gave 2,919 courses to 152,229 students. In addition, the consolidation and improvement of mass education may be measured in qualitative terms.

The curricula of the people's universities reflect the determination not only to cover all the main themes of knowledge, but also to meet the needs of different categories of students. The following synoptic list shows the subjects taught in the people's universities as a percentage and in order of importance: social sciences, 35; economics, 16; foreign languages, 15; natural sciences, 14; literature and art, 9; practical and vocational training, 7; general education, 4.

The increasing popularity that this method of disseminating knowledge is gaining among the different sections of the population may also be seen in the success of the people's universities in rural areas. Considerable progress has been made since 1968/69, when people's universities were opened, on an experimental basis, in several villages. From 56 in 1969/70, the number of people's universities in rural areas has risen to 212—more than half of the total number of such establishments. This phenomenon is all the more noteworthy when we remember that today 59 per cent of the country's population live and work in rural areas. Furthermore, as they penetrate more deeply into the cultural life of towns and villages, the people's universities attract increasing numbers of students from the other national groups. Thus, the 67 people's universities which have been opened in areas where part of the population belongs to these groups provide a total of 192 courses in their own languages—164 in Hungarian and 28 in German. Outstanding among the people's universities is the People's University of Bucharest, which offers 104 courses and lecture series and has more than 10,000 students.

Obviously, a movement of this kind depends on a large degree of participation by all intellectuals. The figures show that 25,000 teachers, members of university scientific councils and heads of departments participate in such work, and in most cases give their services voluntarily. A number of these are persons eminent in science, art, culture, economics or other walks of life.

Amateur artists' groups

Romania has a lively and authentic artistic heritage, the product of the people's creative work throughout the ages. The existence of 24,000 separate groups, with a membership running into hundreds of thousands, shows that the amateur art movement, which offers tremendous scope for the cultivation of the people's talent, has become a mass movement. These groups of amateurs give regular public performances and organize concerts, exhibitions and entertainments in the towns and villages. Competitions are held to stimulate such activities. About 8,500 groups comprising some 200,000 performers competed in the tenth Festival of Music and Dance in 1971, and in the same year more than 5,000 drama groups comprising 100,000 actors took part in the sixth Festival of Amateur Theatre Groups, which bears the name of the great Romanian dramatist I. L. Caragiale. The fourth and fifth National Exhibitions of Folk Art were preceded by local exhibitions of work by 25,000 artists, and the sixth National Exhibition of Amateur Art was preceded by more than 270 local exhibitions in which more than 4,800 amateurs exhibited some 18,000 works of art.

The range of festivals and competitions for amateurs has recently been extended to include a Festival of Amateur Cinema, a Festival of Amateur Photography, a Festival of Puppet Theatre, and regional choral and brass-band festivals. The annual Black Sea Festival of Folk-song, Folk Dancing and National Costume attracts 40 participating groups, which perform before an audience of more than 100,000 Romanians and foreign tourists. Mention should also be made of the many local activities; in almost every district large-scale cultural and artistic events are held at which the traditions and talents of the country's different regions can be appreciated. The State and the different workers' organizations do a great deal to encourage the amateur theatre. In addition to the groups in houses of culture in the towns and cultural centres in the villages, 14 permanent amateur theatre companies produce plays by Romanian dramatists or plays of world repute. A total of 36 people's art schools, with 800 teachers, provide training for thousands of amateurs (approximately 12,000 in 1969/70), including stage directors, conductors of orchestras and choreographers.

The State is particularly generous in its support of creative and highly skilled artists who work in the traditional arts, helping them to maintain the traditions of Romanian folk art, to discover new forms of expression and to pass on the secrets of their skills to the rising generation. Peasant embroidery, ceramics, poker-work and many other products of the people's artistic talents are the subject of exhibitions, fairs and other events which are always highly appreciated.

The Romanian people's reputation for creativity has gone beyond the national frontiers, and the number of invitations from abroad received by art groups is constantly increasing: 4 in 1966, 12 in 1968, 34 in 1969, 35 in 1970, 50 in 1971 and 50 in 1972.

The appreciation of specialists and of the public is reflected in the awards and trophies received by Romanian creative artists: the Collier d'Or (Dijon, France, 1968); the Golden Hatchet (Zakopane, Poland, 1969 and 1970); the Golden Goddess (Ephesus, Turkey, 1969, 1970 and 1972); the Gold Cross and San Mateo (Oviedo, Spain, 1969); the Disque d'Or (France, 1969 and 1970); the Special Prize of the City of Krakow (Poland, 1972); the Golden Bagpipe (Erice, Italy, 1968 and 1969); the First Prize and the Miner's Lamp (Belgium, 1972); the Crystal Bowl and the Grand Prize (Tampere, Finland, 1972); the Disque d'Or and the Grappe d'Or (Dijon, France, 1972); the Crystal Bowl (Zielona Gora, Poland, 1972); and the Achilles Trophy, Gold Medal and Diploma (Agrinion, Greece, 1972).

The Institute of Ethnography and Folklore at Bucharest is concerned with the creative arts of the people and, more generally, with the cultural heritage as a whole seeking to enhance their value and to make them part of contemporary intellectual life. Its activity is centred mainly on important matters such as the ethnographic atlas of Romania, the creative art of the people today, the importance of tradition in contemporary craft work, the national collection of folklore and so on, but it also influences the development of folk culture through direct participation in the various activities carried on throughout the country. In addition, the institute carries out the important task of collecting and recording examples of folklore and ethnographical material which are of national significance. At present, its collections include more than 14,000 wax recordings, more than 8,500 tape recordings, some 11,000 gramophone records and matrices, more than 90,000 items of information from the original sources, approximately 40,000 musical scores and 55,000 photographs and scientific documents. The scientific, cultural and historical value of the institute's collections lies in their absolute authenticity and the scientific methods used to build up and preserve the documentation, rather than the amount of material collected.

Cultural research

An increasing amount of research—sociological, pedagogical, psychological and anthropological—is being done on educational work; it has become the subject of systematic multidisciplinary research.

At a national symposium held in December 1968 on the theme 'Adult Education—Scientific Research and Cultural Action', the theory of adult education and the methodology of research, practical research and the place of tradition in educational work were discussed in detail, and the conclusion was reached that the future development of adult education must have a scientific basis, and that, notwithstanding the complexity of this field of human activity, the gropings of empiricism must give place more and more to rational methods. A number of specialized publications, including the *Pedagogical Review*, the *Cultural Guide*, which also appears in Hungarian (*Müvelödes*) and German (*Volk und Kultur*), *The Club* and others, deal with the problems of adult education and the theoretical and methodological foundations of cultural action.

The Village Museum at Bucharest. The architecture and popular arts of all regions of Romania are represented here.

Mihail Eminescu,
the greatest national poet,
bronze statue by Gheorge Anghel,
Garden of the Atheneul Român.

The new building of the Bucharest National Theatre.

The cultural centre of the trade unions at Oradea.

[*Photos:* Romanian National Commission for Unesco.]

Since 1971, under a five-year plan drawn up as a result of close co-operation between the Council of Socialist Culture and Education and the specialized research institutes, studies have been carried out concerning, on the one hand, the fundamental problems of the role of culture in lifelong education, civic education and aesthetic and scientific education, the network of cultural establishments, the economics of culture, and so on and, on the other hand, such specific problems as the function of cultural centres, houses of culture, museums, libraries, theatres, cinemas and people's universities, the role of the amateur movement and of the creative activity of the people in the modern world, the status of cultural workers, etc.

Mass cultural activity cannot be planned and organized unless social needs, the progress of the Romanian nation and the steadily increasing requirements of the people are taken into account. This is why the five-year plan for Romanian development clearly defines the principles of mass culture, with the aim of modernizing activities in this field and improving them by accentuating their scientific character, enriching their content and avoiding those aspects of cultural activity which are only of value as entertainment, or are unrealistic or purely formal.

Cultural relations with other countries

The foreign policy of Romania, which is based on the main principles of its own social and political system, is aimed at the multilateral development of economic, technological, scientific and cultural exchanges, without discrimination, with all the countries of the world, in a spirit of peaceful coexistence between nations.

Being engaged in carrying out a vast programme of economic construction and evolving a progressive culture, Romania is sincerely attached to the ideals of peace and progress, and does everything possible to satisfy the major aspirations of mankind—disarmament, security, peace and co-operation between States on the basis of mutual respect, national sovereignty and independence, and equality of rights. The State considers that, in the context of international relations, the technological and scientific revolution and the general advancement of culture, active participation in the exchange of scientific, cultural and artistic values is a prerequisite of the progress of every people. In order to create a harmoniously developed society, which is Romania's aim, it is indispensable to be familiar with all genuine advances made in any part of the world and to make them one's own. Needless to say, in adopting its grand design for socialist construction, the Romanian State has no intention of setting itself apart from other peoples; on the contrary, it wishes to broaden its collaboration with them to the greatest possible extent, believing that every nation, whether large or small, has contributed to the enrichment of the world's heritage of culture and civilization, and will continue to do so.

At the present time, Romania maintains cultural relations with more than 111 States, and has concluded cultural co-operation agreements with 63 States. In 1973 137 professional and amateur musical or theatrical groups went on tour abroad. Many professional and amateur folklore groups have been awarded prizes at leading festivals and in all continents. In the last few years musical groups, such as the Madrigal Choir, the symphony orchestras of Bucharest, Cluj, Timişoara and the Romanian Radio and Television Orchestra, have given performances in many concert halls throughout the world. Romanian conductors and soloists, including the violinist Ion Voicu and the singers Ludovic Spiess, Nicolae Herlea, Elena Cernei and Ion Buzea, have taken part in a number of concert and opera seasons. Various theatre companies, including the I. L. Caragiale National Theatre of Bucharest, the Lucia Sturdza Bulandre Theatre of Bucharest, the National Theatre of Cluj and the National Theatre of Jassy, to name but a few, have performed masterpieces from the national and world repertoire during their foreign tours. Romanian theatre groups have been invited to various international festivals, and Romanian producers have been invited to stage plays in a number of countries. In 1973 forty-three foreign groups visited Romania, including actors, musicians and ballet dancers from China, Czechoslovakia, France, German Democratic Republic, Federal Republic of Germany, Greece, Hungary, Italy, Japan, U.S.S.R. and a number of other countries. As a result of exchanges in the field of the plastic arts, under cultural agreements, through arrangements between artists' associations or by means of exhibitions, Romanian works of art have been displayed in all parts of the world. In 1973 alone, some 120 exhibitions of Romanian art were organized abroad, while 30 exhibitions of works by foreign artists were held in Romania.

Romanian films have been shown in many countries of the world, at international festivals of feature films and shorts, films for children, educational or scientific films, and animated cartoons held at Cannes, Moscow, Vienna, Brussels, Montreal, Karlovy Vary, La Plata, Sydney, etc. In 1973 twelve films were awarded fourteen prizes, including the Diploma of Honour of the Jury of the International Festival of Moscow and the Grand Prize of the Festival of Gijon (Spain).

An increasing number of Romanian library works are translated into other languages. Romanian art books can be obtained in any country, as well as scientific and technical works which reflect the achievements of Romanian scientific thought. The works of almost all Romania's leading classical and contemporary authors have been published in many countries, either in individual volumes or in anthologies. Some have been awarded international prizes: Tudor Arghezi, Alexandru Philippide, Zeno Vancea, Zaharia Stancu, Mihai Pop, Constantin Daicoviciu, Virgil Vătăsianu, Franyo Zoltan and Eugen Jebeleanu. Since 1971 seminars have been organized to familiarize translators from Romanian into other languages with the main features of contemporary Romanian literature. Thirty-nine translators from sixteen countries attended the seminar held in 1971.

As part of the programme to strengthen cultural exchanges, a number of 'weeks' or 'days' of Romanian culture have recently been organized in other countries, and similar events have been held in Romania. These events have included exhibitions, film festivals, theatrical performances, folk plays and music recitals. Romanian cultural workers and artists take part in international cultural life by serving on many juries at international competitions and festivals and by making their contribution to the discussions and exchanges of scientific and cultural ideas and values which take place at international meetings and congresses. Eighteen persons, eminent in Romanian cultural affairs, are at present playing a leading role in various international non-governmental organizations concerned with theatre, music, the plastic arts, literature and cinema. Radu Beligan, a people's artist, is president of the International Society for Ethnography and Folklore.

Romania seeks to diversify its cultural exchanges and, in particular, to strengthen its relations with the countries of Africa, Asia and Latin America, whose influence on the development of artistic creation throughout the world and on the general evolution of the modern world is steadily increasing.

The State also promotes the dissemination in Romania of library and other works produced by other peoples. In 1971 448 works of a literary, scientific, socio-political or artistic nature were translated into Romanian, and 12,627,000 copies of these were printed. In 1972 157 feature films and 71 shorts from abroad were screened in Romania; in 1973 the figures were 182 feature films and 97 shorts. Since the beginning of the 1971–72 season, 240 classical and modern plays from abroad have been produced in Romanian theatres.

Training and use
of human resources

The application of any cultural policy depends essentially on the manner in which human resources are involved in such action and on the number of persons taking part in it, but above all on their professional, intellectual and moral qualities. Experience in Romania and elsewhere reveals the complex relationship between cultural development and the standard education system. Thanks to the introduction in 1950–52 of universal elementary education and of compulsory ten-year schooling, and to the fact that almost a quarter of the population enjoys free education in one form or another, an educated public has been created which can appreciate the values of authentic culture, so that the atmosphere is favourable both to the dissemination of culture and to the assertion of new values. Furthermore, the education system, which is adapted to the needs of social development, is now capable of training the specialists required both for cultural and artistic creation and for the dissemination and organization of culture. The major guidelines of State policy concerning training and the use of human resources in the field of culture are the following: (a) the haphazard element in the training of personnel should be eliminated, and the methods of planned development should be applied to it; (b) pluralist educational structures should be adopted which are capable of developing the people's talents to the full, in conformity with the profoundly democratic spirit of the educational system as a whole; (c) the assistance of a large number of voluntary cultural organizers should be enlisted, as well as that of specialists; (d) the principles of lifelong education should be applied, so that people's knowledge can be kept up to date and their abilities cultivated, and so that each person's capacity for self-instruction can be developed.

Art education occupies a leading place among the means employed in the training of the personnel necessary for cultural development. It is planned so as to stimulate the artistic capacities of children, adolescents and adults, and it is provided in schools at the various levels. In 1972–73, sixty-two art schools were in operation, including thirty-four schools of music and plastic arts and twenty-eight secondary schools teaching music, plastic arts and choreography, and there were eleven faculties providing courses in art.

The schools of music and art, which are situated at suitable points throughout the country, give children with artistic talent the opportunity of developing their abilities during the eight-year course. Many of these schools have kindergartens where children of pre-school age receive a special art education. Most of the pupils of these schools continue their studies for a further four years in music and art secondary schools, where, in addition to their specialized studies, they have general education comparable to that provided in the normal secondary schools.

Higher education in the arts is provided in two theatre institutes (one of which has Hungarian as the language of instruction), with sections devoted to theatrical and cinematographic art and to theatrical and film production; in two institutes of plastic arts, which provide training in painting, sculpture, the graphic arts, the history and theory of art, monumental painting, scene-painting, ceramics, glass and metal work, textiles and industrial decoration and aesthetics; and in two *conservatoires* with sections devoted to interpretation, singing, musicology, the training of conductors and the training of teachers. In 1972/73 3,065 students were taking courses of higher education in the arts, the majority (approximately 1,700) were following courses in music. The students receive a broad theoretical training, as may be seen from the sums expended on each student: in 1972/73, almost 39,000 lei per student in the theatre institutes and more than 25,000 lei per student in the institutes of music and art, compared with the average figure of 11,000 lei for each university student—this latter figure itself being relatively high.

Art education, particularly at the higher level, is of a practical nature and seeks from the outset to familiarize pupils and students with the problems which they will encounter in their professional work. Considerable attention is given to precocious talents, which are encouraged by competitions, participation in public performances and the award of scholarships for study abroad.

Drawing and music are taught in all classes throughout the period of compulsory schooling. Future teachers of music and drawing attend teacher-training institutes for three years. The teaching of art subjects in all classes in elementary and secondary schools plays an important role in the education of public taste, and makes it possible to detect talents and to see that gifted children are sent to specialized schools.

A special place in art education is occupied by the thirty people's art schools, which cater for young people and adults, whatever standard they have reached, with the aim of helping them develop their artistic capacities. Attended by thousands of students, these schools, which provide free training in more than forty subjects, are an important factor in the aesthetic education of the people, the stimulation of the amateur art movement and the preservation of folk art traditions. Many outstanding artists began their careers in these schools.

Other cultural workers are trained either in vocational education establishments or in the universities. Training for the very many library workers is provided in a post-secondary school, a daytime school of librarianship and the department of bibliology at the University of Bucharest.

Most of those who work in the creative arts or in the dissemination of culture (men of letters, publishers, sociologists, cultural organizers) receive a university training. Higher education is obligatory for persons occupying specialized posts in cultural work. In a number of faculties (especially those of letters, philosophy and history) syllabuses include both theoretical and practical training, so that the graduates are immediately capable of applying themselves to specific tasks.

Legislation concerning lifelong education was introduced in 1971. Every employee of the State, irrespective of his function and the training he has had, must, during the five years following appointment, undergo some form of further vocational training. He may widen his knowledge by learning to do another job or by acquiring further qualifications in addition to those required for his job in the first place. It is hoped that in this way every employee will keep himself up to date and that weaknesses in the school system will be overcome. Accordingly, in drawing up syllabuses innovations are included in all subjects, students are helped to assimilate new trends of thought and to learn modern techniques. When these 58,000 employees had done their further vocational training in cultural and artistic work, it became necessary, owing to the great variety of their jobs and functions and of their cultural standards, to diversify syllabuses and even to draw up individual programmes of study, group study being used only for categories of persons with common interests. Account is also taken of the fact that vocational education programmes are intended for persons who have already had some professional experience, which makes it desirable to avoid routine and traditional teaching procedures and to make use of modern methodology and techniques.

It is expected that, by 1975, all persons working in cultural and artistic institutions will have done the first part of the vocational retraining course and even that a small proportion of them will have done the second part. The results obtained are reflected in promotions and wage increases.

Voluntary organizers of cultural activities are an important category of those engaged in cultural development. These intellectuals, the 4,500 directors of cultural centres and librarians (in equal numbers), who work in rural areas which are not district centres, lecturers in the people's universities or instructors working with amateur groups, professors, writers, doctors, engineers, civil servants and even students—all these foster the development of local cultural activity in urban and more particularly rural areas. This transfer of ideas, knowledge and experience is profitable to all. Regular short training courses in the methodology of cultural activity are organized for these categories of cultural workers, and enable them to make a more effective contribution to the cultural development of their communities.

Funds allocated to culture and art

Funds for cultural activities are included in annual and long-term plans and in the State budget.

These funds are intended to cover the cost of the normal operation of existing establishments, as well as the smooth development of the network in all parts of the country, particularly in those areas in which there were formerly no cultural and artistic institutions. The funds allocated by the State for the development of culture increase from year to year, as may be seen from the following figures: 1955, 327.1 million lei (taken as a basis of 100); 1960, 529.3 (162); 1965, 738.2 (226); 1970, 921.7 (282); 1971, 981.1 (300); 1972, 998.8 (305); 1973, 1,002.0 (306); 1974 (estimate), 1,039.6 (318).

Most cultural and art establishments are entirely or partially financed by the State, either from the national budget or from the budgets of local administrations. The remaining establishments are financially independent and acquire their resources from their own activities.

The following items of expenditure are entirely financed from the national or local budgets:

The construction of theatres, concert halls and cinemas, library premises, museums, exhibition galleries, etc., the equipment of establishments used for cultural and artistic purposes and the expenses incurred in carrying out major repairs to buildings and equipment (in 1973 alone, new buildings for the I. L. Caragiale National Theatre of Bucharest, the National Theatre of Craiova and the Tîrgu-Mureş Theatre were inaugurated).

The Central Library belonging to the Council of Socialist Culture and Education, the Library of the Academy of the Socialist Republic of Romania (the largest in the country), the central university libraries, libraries in schools and higher educational establishments, as well as the extensive network of libraries in towns and communes, the latter with branches in the villages of each commune.

Museums of all kinds, including memorial museums; the organization of art exhibitions in Romania and abroad; the participation of Romania in international fairs and exhibitions.

Royalties; the erection of statues, busts and monuments in public squares; the decoration of important buildings; supplying museums and other State and public institutions with works of art by contemporary Romanian artists.

Research and the presentation, for scientific purposes and for tourism, of historic and artistic monuments, both secular and religious, throughout the country, together with the emergency action necessary for the preservation of these monuments.

The special training centre for the staff of the Institute of Ethnography and Folklore; the artistic movement among the people; the people's art schools in each district; training centres for amateurs in each district, and broadcasting stations in towns and villages.

The organization of national and international cultural and artistic events, and participation in the different cultural and artistic events organized in other countries.

Houses of culture and cultural centres (salaries, maintenance, furnishings).

The following establishments are partially financed by the State:

Theatres, opera and operetta houses, philharmonic orchestras, symphony orchestras, folklore groups, puppet theatres, concert halls and variety theatres and the State circus, all of which receive the difference between their income from the sale of tickets and their expenditure on salaries and consultants' fees (which account for 80 per cent of their costs), décors, costumes, the maintenance of premises and travel. It should be pointed out that the subsidy provided by the State amounts to 75–90 per cent of total expenditure, which enables companies to keep up a good standard of repertoire and to present programmes of real artistic worth. The importance accorded to the above-mentioned establishments is revealed by the fact that the subsidies they receive account for a third of the total outlay on cultural affairs financed from the State budget.

The Council of Socialist Culture and Education and the local committees for socialist culture and education receive State subsidies to cover any part of the cost of cultural and artistic publications which they cannot meet from their own incomes.

It should be pointed out that the increase in the number of cultural and artistic publications is accompanied by an over-all increase in the number of copies printed, and this enables the State subsidy to be progressively reduced.

The following establishments are self-financing: cinema studios, cinemas and film-distribution companies, radio and television, the recording company Electrecord, the Romanian Agency for Artistic Impresarios (ARIA).

In view of the fact that the average cost of admission to cinemas is 2 lei it may be asked how cinemas manage to make ends meet. The answer is that the State provides assistance in the form of fiscal advantages, aid for investment, etc.

Certain types of establishment, entirely financed by the State, such as museums, houses of culture and cultural centres, also obtain income from their own activities (entry tickets to museums, sale of publications, entry tickets to artistic events, rental for halls, etc.), which they may use directly so that they can carry out their tasks under the best possible conditions.

Certain creative artists' unions, such as the Writers' Union and the Composers' Union, are not subsidized by the State, whilst the Union of Plastic Artists does receive a subsidy. Creative artists' unions spend a lot of money on the publication of their reviews (the Writers' Union, for example, publishes eleven reviews), retirement and disability pensions and pensions paid to the descendants of eminent persons, the development of documentation, convalescent homes, creative workshops, etc. Their financial resources come from the subscriptions of their members, and from copyright fees, and they also receive a certain amount of State assistance. The Writers' Union, for instance, receives 0.70 lei for each book sold (this sum being included in the sale price), and 10 per cent of royalties from publishing houses and places of entertainment.

It should also be noted that, in addition to cultural establishments built with the aid of investment funds allocated by the State, a large number of cultural establishments are built each year thanks to the people's contribution in the form of money labour. Thus, during the last ten years, 2,170 cultural centres have been built in rural areas—an example of the socially useful labour carried out voluntarily by the citizens in the various districts in order to modernize and beautify their surroundings. A committee of the Council of Socialist Culture and Education is at present preparing cultural development plans up to the year 2000, taking account of the cultural level which it is hoped that the population will attain by the end of this century and of the efforts which the State must undertake to achieve the desired objectives.

Appendix

The Constitution of the Socialist Republic of Romania (extracts)

In the Socialist Republic of Romania, the entire activity of the State is aimed at consolidating the régime, strengthening the socialist nation, increasing the material welfare of the people and raising their cultural level, ensuring the freedom and dignity of man and promoting the assertion of the human personality. To this end, the Romanian Socialist State:

Article 13
Develops education at all levels, provides the necessary conditions for the development of science, the arts and culture, and sees to the protection of the people's health.

Article 17
The citizens of the Socialist Republic of Romania, irrespective of nationality, race, sex or religion, have equal rights in all fields of economic, political, juridical, social and cultural life. The State guarantees the equality of citizens' rights. No limitation of these rights is permitted and no discrimination in the exercise of these rights, on the grounds of nationality, race, sex or religion, is allowed.

Any act, the aim of which is to impose such limitations, and any nationalistic propaganda or incitement to racial or nationalistic hatred are punishable by law.

Article 22
National groups in the Socialist Republic of Romania are entitled to use their mother tongue freely, and to have books, newspapers, magazines, theatrical performances and education at all levels in their mother tongue. In administrative units inhabited by people whose nationality is other than Romanian, all bodies and institutions must use that nationality's language, both orally and in writing, and must appoint officials who are of that nationality or who are familiar with its language and with the way of life of the local population.

Statement issued at the tenth Congress of the Romanian Communist Party (1969) (extracts)

Our Party, which promotes a policy receptive of all the values of world culture, considers that it is the duty of Romanian creative artists and writers to interpret the genius of our people at all times and to reflect in their work the specific nature of Socialist society. Thus they will be able to make an effective contribution to the assertion of national values in world culture. . . .

. . . the Party and the State highly esteem art and literature as important factors in knowledge, which can influence people's thoughts and feelings, and consider that they can play an important part in the development of a Socialist consciousness and in the elevation of the spiritual level of mankind.

**Speech by Nicolae Ceauşescu,
President of the Council of State
of the Socialist Republic of Romania,
General Secretary
of the Romanian Communist Party**

. . . in establishing the main lines of development of education, science and culture . . . the Party takes account of the specific character of our country. Experience shows that neglect of this factor has undesirable consequences for the development of the intellectual life of society. (1967.)

. . . accomplishing its historic mission in Romania, the Communist Party takes it as a principle that science and culture are components of the process of Socialist and Communist construction of the country. The propagation of science and culture among the people and the improvement of the level of general knowledge of all are necessary if our society is to reach the higher stage represented by Communism, and if men are to be enabled to release, in increasing abundance, the material and spiritual wealth of our country. It is only by constantly strenghening art and culture and by disseminating them among the people that we can accelerate the process of eradicating the mentality of the past and raising the Socialist consciousness of the workers. (1968.)

Man in a Socialist society seeks to act wittingly in the sphere of intellectual creation; it is his intention to create a culture which is not the fruit of a casual activity but springs from an enlightened sense of necessity, a new culture drawing its inspiration from the realism of the new society from socialist devotion to human interests, a culture dedicated to the people and to the people alone. (1968.)

. . . the Party and the State are encouraging the free development of artists of all kinds, and are promoting research and artistic experiments undertaken on a vast scale . . . with a view to enriching the palette of our modern art.

. . . the problem of cultural and artistic activity conducted in the mother tongue should be considered from the point of view of the content of such activity. We must create all the necessary conditions for men to organize their cultural and artistic activities in the language with which they are most familiar; but we must see to it that this has a unifying, not a divisive effect, and that it contributes to strengthening friendship between workers, whether in factories or institutions, villages or towns, irrespective of their nationality. Although our cultural activity makes use of different tongues, it must ultimately enable us, as it were, to speak a single language: the language of Communism. . . . (1971.)

We wish to import those literary and artistic works which are likely to broaden the horizon of the workers and have something to tell us about the struggle waged by other peoples in furtherance of social progress and peace. We wish to export our own artistic products in order to make others familiar with our endeavours and with our new way of life. The exchange of cultural values with other countries will thus contribute to a better understanding between peoples, to the development of their collaboration and friendship, to the establishment of world peace. Such is the mission of true art, and we approve of cultural exchanges of this kind; in this way, we are serving both the interests of our people and the cause of progress throughout the world. (1971.)

Decree No. 301 of 15 September 1971
on the creation, organization and functions
of the Council of Socialist Culture and Education

Article 1
There is hereby established a Council of Socialist Culture and Education, which shall operate as an organ of the Party and the State coming directly under the Central Committee of the Romanian Communist Party and the Council of Ministers, to be responsible for applying Party and State policy in the field of socialist culture and education, and for laying down guidelines for all cultural and educational activities undertaken in the Socialist Republic of Romania.

Article 3
The functions of the Council of Socialist Culture and Education shall be as follows:

(a) It shall initiate activities designed to stimulate literary and artistic creativity, giving prominence to works produced in the fields of literature, the cinema, the theatre, music and the visual arts which are imbued with a militant spirit and thus serve the interests of the people and of socialist society; it shall also promote a critical appreciation of the nation's cultural heritage.

(b) It shall be responsible for ensuring that the policies of artistic institutions of all kinds throughout the country meet the educational requirements of Romanian society.

(c) It shall be responsible for ensuring that the ideological and artistic tendencies of nationally produced films as well as the system of distribution of films throughout the Socialist Republic of Romania, are in conformity with the cultural policy of the Party and the State.

(d) It shall approve the subject programmes of publishing houses and supervise their activity; it shall be responsible for guiding and organizing the production and dissemination of books in Romania with the aim of broadening the socialist cultural horizon of the workers.

(e) It shall direct the work of all cultural establishments (clubs, houses of culture, cultural centres, libraries, etc.), irrespective of the organizations to which they belong (people's councils, trade unions, UCECOM, CENTROCOOP, etc.), in such a way as to ensure that they undertake large-scale activities with a view to providing the working masses in towns and villages with information about the domestic and foreign policy of the Party and about successes achieved in the construction of socialism; that they give wide publicity to whatever is new and advanced in contemporary culture, science and technology; and that they actively promote belief in the principles of socialist philosophy and ethics and foster a progressive public-spirited attitude among the masses with the aim of educating their socialist consciousness; it shall stimulate the artistic creativity of the people and the development of modern folklore, and shall highlight the richness of Romania's folk art.

(f) It shall direct, guide and supervise all publication activities related to culture, literature and the arts, ensuring that they effectively promote the philosophy and aesthetics of dialectical materialism and the cultural policy of the Romanian Communist Party; it shall encourage artists to participate in the social and political life of the country.

(g) It shall organize and guide such activities as are likely to facilitate the study, conservation and protection of buildings of historical, artistic and architectural interest throughout the country, and shall draw attention to their value for scientific research, the patriotic education of the population and the development of tourism.

(h) In the spirit of peace and friendship with all peoples which characterizes the foreign policy of the Romanian State, the Council of Socialist Culture and Education shall strive to develop cultural co-operation between Romania and the socialist countries, the developing countries and all the other countries of the world, with a view to extending contacts and co-operation between the cultural authorities of Romania and progressive intellectual circles everywhere, and to ensuring the active participation of Romania in international artistic and cultural life. The Council of Socialist Culture and Education shall make the whole world familiar with the cultural creativity and artistic genius of the Romanian people, the representative works of all kinds it has produced, and the great cultural achievements of socialist Romania; at the same time, it shall ensure that the cultural and artistic achievements of other peoples and the progressive works which are created in every part of the world and serve as vehicles of great humanist ideals, are widely known in our country. To this end, it shall organize artistic and cultural exchanges with similar bodies and establishments in other countries, as well as the activity of impresarios concerned with artistic activities.

(i) It shall apply an equitable policy of selection and promotion of personnel working in its field of action and shall provide ideological and vocational training for the staff of cultural establishments; it shall be jointly responsible with the Ministry of Education for the activities of establishments of artistic education.

(j) Assisted by the creative artists' unions and by ministries and other central and local administrative bodies, it shall ensure that funds allocated for cultural purposes are employed to promote socialist, revolutionary and progressive art, and to acquire and disseminate works serving the interests and meeting the requirements of Romania's socialist society.

(k) It shall approve the creation or dissolution of cultural and artistic establishments coming under ministries, other central bodies, and the executive committees of district people's councils or of Bucharest municipal councils.

Article 4

The Council of Socialist Culture and Education shall organize and supervise the nation-wide implementation of decisions taken by the Party and the State on cultural matters.

Article 5

The Council of Socialist Culture and Education shall prepare studies and analyses relating to its field of competence, and shall submit to the Central Committee of the Romanian Communist Party and to the Council of Ministers proposals for the improvement of cultural and educational activity and the development of the network of artistic and cultural establishments, together with suggestions concerning the material basis of cultural life in Romania.

70